Mingled Voices 7

International Proverse Poetry Prize Anthology 2022

Proverse Hong Kong

2023

MINGLED VOICES 7 contains the work of fifty-one poets. The one hundred or so poems were selected from those entered for the International Proverse Poetry Prize in 2022, the seventh such annual international competition administered from Hong Kong.

The International Proverse Poetry Prize was jointly founded in 2016 by Dr Gillian Bickley and Dr Verner Bickley, MBE, in association with the annual international Proverse Prize for unpublished book-length fiction, non-fiction or poetry, submitted in English, which they also founded, in 2008.

Poems could be submitted on any subject or topic, chosen by each poet, or on the subject selected for 2022 by the Administrators, "Renewal" (interpreted in any way each writer chose). There was a free choice of interpretation, form and style.

Included in the anthology are the poems that won the first, second, and third prizes. Selection to appear in the anthology was also awarded as a prize by the judges. This year, special mention is additionally made of five of these poets.

Poems were submitted from around the world by writers with a variety of previous writing experience.

Brief biographies of all of those whose work is represented in *Mingled Voices 7* are included in the anthology as well as authors' background notes on their work.

Supported by

Hong Kong Arts Development Council fully supports freedom of artistic expression. The views and opinions expressed in this project do not represent the stand of the Council.

MINGLED VOICES 7
INTERNATIONAL PROVERSE POETRY PRIZE
ANTHOLOGY 2022

Poets

Vinita Agrawal · Joy Al-Sofi · Shikha Bansal ·
Alan Bern · Maria Elena Blanco · Gavin Bourke ·
Lawrence Bridges · Lina Buividaviciute ·
Sean Camshon · Carol Flake Chapman · Tom Choi ·
William Leo Coakley · Suzanne Cottrell · Julio Diaz ·
Neil Douglas · Ahmed Elbeshlawy · Dean Gessie ·
Olga Gonzalez Latapi · Casey Hampton ·
Sadie Kaye · Zachary Knox · Gary Lai · Ho Cheung Lee ·
Sharon Ludan · K B Ryan Joshua Mahindapala ·
Carmina Masoliver · Wayne Paul Mattingly ·
Jack Mayer · Lily Mayo · Terry Miller · Keith Nunes ·
Denise O'Hagan · Helen Oliver · Rena Ong · Jun Pan ·
Joanna Radwańska-Williams · kerry rawlinson ·
M. Ann Reed · Vinni Relwani ·
Allegra Jostad Silberstein · Wesley Sims ·
Hayley Solomon · Abbie Taylor ·
Luisa Ternau · Edward Tiesse · Roger Uren ·
Anna Verhaegh · Kewayne Wadley · Honghua Wang ·
George Watt · Michael Witts

Editors

Gillian Bickley · Verner Bickley

Proverse Hong Kong

Mingled Voices 7
International Proverse Poetry Prize Anthology 2022
edited by Gillian Bickley and Verner Bickley.
First published in Hong Kong by Proverse Hong Kong,
27 April 2023.
Paperback edition, ISBN-13: 978-988-8833-38-2
Ebook edition, ISBN-13: 978-988-8833-39-9

Distribution (Hong Kong and worldwide):
The Chinese University of Hong Kong Press,
The Chinese University of Hong Kong,
Shatin, New Territories, Hong Kong SAR.
E-mail: cup-bus@cuhk.edu.hk; Web: www.cup.cuhk.edu.hk
Proverse page: https://cup.cuhk.edu.hk/Proversehk
Distribution (United Kingdom)
Stephen Inman, Worcester, UK.
Enquiries to:
Proverse Hong Kong, P.O. Box 259, Tung Chung Post Office,
Tung Chung, Lantau, NT, Hong Kong SAR, China.
E-mail: proverse@netvigator.com;
Web: https://www.proversepublishers.com

Page design by Proverse Hong Kong.
Cover design by Pin-Key Design Co.
Cover image, 'Hong Kong Storm' by Kasra Shroff.

British Library Cataloguing in Publication Data.
A catalogue record for this book is available
from the British Library.

MINGLED VOICES 7
TABLE OF CONTENTS

POEMS

ACKNOWLEDGEMENTS

All those at Proverse Hong Kong, administrators of the Proverse Poetry Prize (single poems), thank all those who entered for the 2022 competition, and warmly appreciate the helpful and willing participation in the editorial process of those whose poems were selected for this anthology.

We are most grateful, also, for the professionalism and dedication of the judges.

The Hotel Coma, Ordino, Principat d'Andorra, is warmly thanked for its always willing and friendly help with practicalities in the past, which we are sure will resume once travel restrictions make it possible for the judging panel to travel and meet there again.

On this occasion, we give particular thanks to Joanna Radwańska-Williams, first-prize winner of the Proverse Poetry Prize 2021, for her opening Message and to Jeff Streeter for his Preface.

We are most grateful to the editors of the Journal of Postcolonial Writing for accepting and working with us to publish an article on the Proverse Prize:
https://www.tandfonline.com/eprint/TKVG8HZSZWX6R4CUJ UKM/full?target=10.1080/17449855.2022.2101653

LOOKING FORWARD TO THE NEXT COMPETITION
THE INTERNATIONAL
PROVERSE POETRY PRIZE 2023

We very much hope that <u>all who entered</u> for the Proverse Poetry Prize 2022, not only those who won a place in *Mingled Voices 7: Proverse Poetry Prize Anthology 2022* but also of course <u>including those anthologised here,</u> will continue to enter their work in future years. We continue to welcome all those who have entered for the Prize since its inauguration in 2016, and all those who were awarded a place or places in previous International Proverse Poetry Prize Anthologies in the *Mingled Voices* series. It is a pleasure to recognize as repeat entrants the names of those who have entered before and to compare and contrast their current entry or entries with what we have seen before. We are also always very pleased to see new names and we hope that there will be more new entrants in 2023 and beyond.

Receipt of entries for the 2023 competition begins on 7 May 2023 with 30 June 2023 as the deadline.

As in previous years, poets may enter poems either on a subject or theme of their own choice or on the theme suggested by the Administrators for 2023, 'Space', interpreted as each poet may wish. Full and updated details will usually be available on the Proverse website, proversepublishing.com.

In the meantime, we hope that those whose poems are included in the 2023 International Proverse Poetry Prize Anthology will enjoy seeing their and others' work and that all their readers will share the pleasure of the judges and the editors in these "Mingled Voices".

Gillian and Verner Bickley
Hong Kong

NOTE FROM THE EDITORS
and Proverse Poetry Prize Administrators

For this, the seventh annual international Proverse Poetry Prize, poems were invited, either on the entrant's own choice of subject or theme, or on a subject selected by the Proverse Poetry Prize Administrators, "Renewal" (interpreted as each entrant might wish). Any form, style or genre could be used.

Poems were judged by the panel of judges as submitted and the following awards were made:

First Prize
Lina Buividaviciute,
'In November. And the clouds will gather'

Second Prize
Denise O'Hagan, 'Pietà'

Third Prizes
Carol Flake Chapman, 'Resurrection'
Suzanne Cottrell, 'Haven Among Trees'
Joanna Radwańska-Williams, 'How the Fish Feel'
George Watt, 'Boy in a Boat'

Specially Mentioned
'Stroke' by Vinita Agrawal
'renewal' by Dean Gessie
'Or So Says the Wind' by Casey Hampton
'Epiphany' by Allegra Jostad Silberstein
'Watching the Dusk on a Rainy Night: Musing'
by Luisa Ternau

Several other entered poems were awarded a place in this International Proverse Poetry Prize Anthology 2022,
Mingled Voices 7.
Their names appear in the Table of Contents
as well as on the title page.

Congratulations to all!

A small number of the poems in the Anthology were edited by or in consultation with the writers after selection for the Anthology and before publication, but no further judging of the entries was made at this stage.

All writers were invited to contribute a commentary and/or notes on their poems, to be included in this anthology, and have responded in different ways.

Brief biographies of all those whose work is represented in *Mingled Voices 7* can be found towards the back of the anthology.

To the extent that those whose poetry is published here tell us about their occupations and/or working lives, we know that among them (the following description is not exhaustive) are <u>authors and writers</u> (including of advertising materials, ESL (English as a Second Language) materials, historical romance and non-fiction, and in the areas of advertising and game invention), editors including of literary magazines, essayists, literary critics, novelists, playwrights, poets, researchers, writers for radio, translators / revisers (including of French, German, Spanish, and poetry), <u>current, former and retired librarians</u>, <u>current, former and retired teachers and professors</u> at different levels and for different groups in different areas, including Comparative Culture, Interpretation, Languages (including English and French), Literary and Comparative Studies, Literature (English and French), Linguistics (Slavic and English), Translation), Organic Unity Study of Literatures. More than one has worked in <u>publishing</u> for a number of years and one or two have founded their own press; at least one is <u>on the advisory board of a national poetry prize</u>. <u>Others are, for example</u>, an American Foreign Service Officer, a retired Australian diplomat, a film-maker, a game-inventor, a homemaker, doctors in general practice, a farmer, a film-maker, a former practicing attorney, a radio writer/performer.

Again, to the extent that those who hold degrees make explicit mention of them (and not all do), we know that among them they hold degrees (including at Bachelor's, Master's and PhD levels) in, among others, creative writing, English and Linguistics, English Literature, Humanities, Librarianship and Information Studies, Law, Lithuanian philology and advertising, Lithuanian literature, Writing. One has a DPhil in

Social and Cultural Anthropology. At least one is still undergoing formal education.

Poems were submitted from Australia, Chile, Hong Kong, India, Ireland, Lithuania, Macau, New Zealand, Singapore, the United Kingdom and the United States of America.

The known or presumed countries of birth of these poets include Australia, Cuba, Egypt, Hong Kong, India, Ireland, Italy, New Zealand, Poland, South Africa, Singapore, the United Kingdom and the United States of America.

Some are new or young writers. Others are already well-published as poets, whether in magazines and journals or in book form, some with several published poetry collections of their own. Some are prize-winning writers and/or winners of grants to support their literary work. Several have participated as poets (and in one case as a panel moderator) in national and international poetry festivals and other prestigious events. Some are leaders in that they have formed poetry writing and/or appreciation groups, including online writing communities. At least one is on the advisory board for a literary prize; one has judged poetry contests. One or two are widely translated.

For some of the poets, English is not their mother-tongue. About twenty-four are men and about twenty-seven are women.

* * *

Entrants were asked to submit their work in English. To qualify, entries needed to be previously unpublished in English, but could have been previously published in another language.

Poems were invited in any genre, form, or style. Nearly all are in free verse; although a small number use specific forms, which may be signaled by the title of a poem, as with Denise O'Hagan's 'The orphan's pantoum'. In another case, a helpful note or backstory gives us the clue. For example, kerry rawlinson explains that her poem, 'we few', "is a mirror poem, reflecting (in a literal sense) on who or what institutions or entities control us. As with most things in life, often a different viewpoint offers a completely novel experience; an opening; a way forward. Sometimes, as in the poem's title, life is a palindrome and turns out the same whether you experience it forwards—or backwards." Among Joy Al-Sofi's poems, one is a group of haikus. Casey Hampton describes his poem, 'Sarah Van Fleet Come Dawn' as, "an example of nesting poetry … the practice of combining multiple poems of the same form, sharing a common theme, into a single poem, while honoring the original form, in this case, the Haiku." One poet is not sure whether her poem is a prose poem or simply a poem.

Most of the poems, but not all, are in free verse. Poetic techniques include, for example, enjambement, rhyme, repetition (movingly used in Vinni Relwani's 'I Didn't Know the Last Time was the Last Time' and pragmatically in Shikha Bansal's 'A wish for my old age'), mirroring, contradiction ('Unfolding 2022'). The metaphors are sometimes deeply sophisticated as in Casey Hampton's, 'Or So Says the Wind'.

As in previous years, perhaps most are written in the voice of the writer, who may seem to present their own ideas, experiences or feelings. In 'How the Fish Feel', Joanna Radwańska-Williams imagines, with detailed empathy what it might be like to live in a different form as a member of a different species. At least a degree of magic realism strikes us in Maria Elena Blanco's 'Out of the Blue Sea of Letters' and in Julio Diaz's, 'Body Full of Heatstroke'. Lawrence Bridges, 'Any Thing' describes a series of daylight visions. At least one is a "found" poem (Neil Douglas's '7 miles high'). None are identified, as in some previous years, as written in response to comments made during a creative writing workshop.

As always, the anthology as a whole displays a wide range of subjects, situations, events, arguments, thoughts, moods and emotions. The tone ranges from elegiac to analytical, with an occasional touch of humour.

The optional subject selected by the Proverse Poetry Prize Administrators for 2022 was "Renewal" (interpreted as each writer might desire). The season of spring is a clear expression of renewal as found in several poems, including Allegra Jostad Silberstein's 'Epiphany' and Helen Oliver's 'Matariki'. A cluster of poems celebrates the closely-related ideas inspired by trees (Suzanne Cottrell's 'Haven among Trees' and Jack Mayer's 'You Trees'). And there are poems showing a definite movement from urban to country interests (for example, Joy Al-Sofi's, 'Another Overcast Day'). Carol Flake Chapman's 'Resurrection' uses the Egyptian myth of Isis and Osiris to emphasise that renewal is balanced by the loss and pain which hopefully in time will be replaced by renewal. George Watt's, 'Boy in a Boat' relates the transformational power of an innocent. The same poet's 'Lot & his daughters' considers an Old Testament story, which demonstrates that renewal sometimes requires the intervention of action which is usually forbidden by the norms of society. Acts of creation, as in Tom Choi's 'Paper Crane' are themselves forms of renewal.

Some of the poems describe rather the loss and sadness that precede the renewal of joy (e.g. Vinita Agrawal's 'Stroke', Vinni Relwani's 'I Didn't Know the Last Time was the Last Time'). William Leo Coakley's 'Full Moon In Another Country' suggests that change can be a form of renewal or at least provide an opportunity for renewal. On the other hand, Wayne Mattingly's 'Ocean Beach' describes a change which is sadly irreversible, as do several of Joy Al-Sofi's poems, for example, 'Once Was'.

The concept of renewal led to related ideas: the need for personal survival (Lina Buividaviciute's 'About the Legs', Sharon Ludan's 'A Birthday Meditation'), the need to secure the survival of the species and prevent the degradation of planet earth (Edward Tiesse, 'Upsala Glacier' and K B Ryan Joshua Mahindapala, 'A wasteland of arrows'). Roger Uren, in 'A Shakespearean Insight' identifies as obstacles to achieving these goals single individuals who want to demonstrate their complete and universal power. Both William Leo Coakley's 'Music in the Air' and Lily Mayo's 'Music' claim its healing power; while Abbie Taylor's 'Alone in Germany' as well as Maria Elena Blanco's 'Out of the Blue Sea of Letters' allude to the solace provided by the acts of writing and reading. Wesley Sims' 'Recovery and Renewal' is a sensitive account of the gradual restoration of feelings of self-worth in victims of rape.

The word, "renewal" is incorporated in two poem titles, while a related word, "transmogrification", appears in one title. Apart from these titles, the word, "renewal", occurs a mere three times in the anthologized poems as a whole, although, with its reference to the phoenix and its mythical ability to regenerate itself, Helen Oliver's 'reflections at the end of the day' brings the concept of renewal to mind.

Poems on self-chosen topics speak of personal experiences (self-questioning, the search for a job and self-identity (Zachary Knox's 'youth's decadence'); the frustrations of using failing technical aids in teaching (Ho Cheung Lee's 'Machu Picchu'); an online relationship ('Five photos of Diana' – and isn't interesting that we immediately (wrongly) assume that the Diana in question is the late Princess Diana?), the purchase in an Irish market and then the restoration of an old Chinese clock. Some give affectionate portrayals of individuals the poet has known or met (Neil Douglas, 'Geography Teacher', George Watt, 'Boy on a Boat'). Another George Watt poem ('The Waiting Room') enshrines the long-ago intense romantic experience of a young man. Sadie Kaye reflects on bi-polar experiences ('Tidal Slave') and Wayne Paul Mattingly on epilepsy ('Aura'). Carmina Masoliver contemplates a fuller figure ('What would Marie Kondo do') and Abbie Taylor shares one sweet success for a visually challenged young woman ('In the Bowling Alley'). Some respond to personalities and events which have attracted international attention—Julian Asonge, Prity Patel, the present War in Ukraine and the former War in Iraq. As elucidated by his back-story, Keith Nunes talks about the impact on those who view them, both in reality and at second hand, of the various ills in and of the world ('The day I see every day'), while Lina Buividaviciute describes the worries experienced by the mothers of military age sons ('A Letter to My Child of War').

Two poems retell biblical stories (Lina Buividaviciute's 'Potiphar's Wife' and George Watt's 'Lot & His Daughters'), while Denise O'Hagan's 'Pietà' reflects the New Testament story of the Crucifixion of Christ, through its response to a sculpture of the Virgin Mary mourning over the body of her son.

Sharon Ludan ('And the Universe Responds') asserts and accepts that the individual alone is responsible for the conduct and outcome of their life. Shikha Bansal's, 'A wish for my old age' expresses a calm philosophy, while Dean Gessie's, 'Renewal' gives a version of utopia. In one of her poems, Helen Oliver considers the survival of personality ('The Soul') and in another, suggests that personal physical and psychological needs can never be met ('Never enough'). Luisa Ternau presents past pain as the seedbed for future joy ('Watching the Dusk on a rainy night').

A handful are intertextual. Sharon Ludan responds to her own poem as included in an earlier *Mingled Voices* anthology. Some are ekphrastic, inspired by other written works including both religious texts and novels, by woodblock art (Michael Witts' 'Of the Floating World'), or a sculpture (e.g. Denise O'Hagan's 'Pieta'). Lina Buividaviciute in particular shows she finds consistent inspiration in the works of others. Alan Bern ('Once Again: The Courage of Everyday Life') quotes Martin Luther King to introduce his admiration of physically-challenged readers whom he witnessed while a librarian.

This is an international collection derived from an international competition. However, it is administered from Hong Kong and some of the poems give glimpses of Hong Kong life not usually witnessed or experienced by a casual visitor or tourist. Joy Al-Sofi gives a picture of Hong Kong as it was when she first arrived and, in contrast, what mobile phones, Covid-19 and administrative measures have made it. Tom Choi describes both the morning commute and the pastime provided by the Japanese art of origami. Neil Douglas, a regular visitor, with a Hong Kong-born wife, writes about Hong Kong icon, Bruce Lee. Sadie Kaye sketches aspects of her own life in Hong Kong. Ho Cheung Lee reacts to personal events and Hong Kong social customs, and draws a picture of how a fairly typical Hong Kong boy (probably not dissimilar from any boy in the world, fascinated by what new media enable him to create) might spend his day. Honghua Wang's two poems are alive with Hong Kong culture too.

Each poem was judged on its own merits and those selected for this anthology are arranged simply in alphabetical order of poets' surnames and (where more than one poem by a single poet is included) also by title (unless a different sequence was requested by the poet concerned). The poets' commentaries and notes on their poems, requested by the prize administrators to help the international readership, are presented as endnotes. (This year, back-stories and notes were requested at the same time as each poem was entered, rather than, as previously, during the editing process.) The brief biographies of the poets (which were not known to the judges at the time of judging) appear, as supplied by the poets themselves, in alphabetical order of surname.

* * *

All poets have shown considerable commitment to their participation in this anthology. At least a few faced more than usual difficulties in doing so. Some were hindered by extreme weather, others by the impact of Covid-19.

As last year, we deeply appreciate the consideration and conscientiousness which has been demonstrated and wish everyone, their loved ones and families, a safe outcome and renewal from present trials.

Gillian and Verner Bickley
Hong Kong
March 2023

ADVANCE COMMENTARY

The notion of renewal, etymologically, suggests: to flourish once more. The newest edition of *Mingled Voices* takes a lyrical approach to this universal theme, centering on renewal not as a terminus. Rather, renewal centers on a possibility informing the felt reality of each poet in the collection.

Lina Buividaviciute's poem, 'And the clouds will gather,' musters this query in the context of a contemporary setting where in her poem, an autumnal "fog" settles over the speaker's seasonal irritability. This obtuse layer becomes an edge upon which the poem turns, culminating with the speaker's ecstatic "survival" for yet another season.

Denise O'Hagan's 'Pietà,' likewise envisions resistance as a pivotal turn towards rebirth and replenishment where there is almost a magical conjunction between "granite" and "tenderness." The Virgin Mary becomes in the poet's recapitulation the incarnation of mothers fated to survive their progeny. In a poem, at the heart of the collection, Joanna Radwańska-Williams playfully catches a question, jarring to both the attentive fisherman and poet: "how does a fish feel?" Well, how does it feel? Within the fibrous scope of the imagination, the fish feels all senses of emotion from anxiety to the pleasure aroused by satisfying supper until the speaker of her lyric devours the self—and is renewed.

At this juncture, my readings form beginnings in a spring in Zhuhai that, with its grayish film, feels like autumn. Such is the nature of renewal. You are invited in a seasonal spirit to read and enjoy this annual collection—to "celebrate", as Buividaviciute writes, your own discoveries.

Charles Lowe, PhD
Associate Professor
Head, Department of Languages and Cultures
Division of Humanities and Social Sciences
United International College
Zhuhai
PRC

PREFACE BY JEFF STREETER

Previous springs have brought us a dazzling miscellany of poetry in the form of *Mingled Voices* and, happily, this year is no exception, with another batch of freshly hatched poems before us, blinking in the early sunlight of our eager gaze.

As you may have already read, this year's topic was "Renewal"; as with themes from previous years, this one was interpreted widely, though the term takes on a special meaning in the light of our global recovery from the pandemic. However, it also suggests the phrase "Make It New" which, popularised by American poet and critic Ezra Pound, and often quoted in discussions of Modernist poetics, actually seems to have <u>a pedigree dating back to the Shang Dynasty in China</u>. And, I believe, the best of the writing here truly helps us to see the world afresh through the eyes—and above all through the vivid imagination and vibrant words—of the poets.

Compared to last year and much to my relief, the poets generally seem to have got out more. In Hong Kong, at least, they certainly made it as far as the local underground station, with station names cropping up here and there— for instance in Ho Cheung Lee's poignant "Moonlight". And then we find Joy Al-Sofi wondering what she will miss about the city, wryly noting:

> "The MTR is one, of course.
> The way it moves, the sway.
> Six seats of separation
> Where once was chatter-filled full
> Of life and socializing.
> Now all heads bow before the iPhone altar."
> ('Leaving')

And the sights and sounds of nature are scattered throughout the volume too. There are barbets, bulbuls, coucals and more in Al-Sofi's 'Afternoon Haikus', taking me back to my own walks in the hills of Hong Kong Island, so full of birdsong.

Then there are the narcissus and daffodils in Allegra Jostad Silberstein's haunting 'Epiphany'. Such very particular mentions of birds, plants seem to me to be very much in the tradition of the English Romantic poets who took these details seriously. They often wrote about beautiful rural landscapes as a source of joy, making nature poetry a popular poetic genre, though they also pondered the relationship between humanity (they would have said "Man") and nature. Nowadays, as the Critic Jay Parini has pointed out, that relationship is "a pressing political question, a question of survival". (See the introduction of: <u>Poems for a Small Planet: Contemporary American Nature Poetry</u>). We see this in Edward Tiesse's taut 'Upsala Glacier' where the glacier itself is just a "carcass", left "gasping" and which

> surrenders and leaves
> stones for the earth and
> tears for me

A similar note is picked up in Neil Douglas's excellent "Geography Teacher" which cleverly combines a nostalgic wander through memories of geography lessons at school with an uncanny sense of what has been going horribly wrong:

> Then an oxbow lake adrift
> From apathetic silt
> Now a rock-strewn summit
> Eroded by fast glacial melt

There is a sense of things going wrong, too, in Suzanne Cottrell's moving 'Haven Among Trees' where human concerns such as "obligations, debts, illness" are set against the distress calls of the trees, leading to the invocation of a kind of mutual dependency:

> woods nurture and awaken
> my conscience to act and respond
> to your distress calls and to mine
> in the hope of saving each other

A different kind of interdependency is explored in 'How The Fish Feel' as Joanna Radwańska-Williams wittily gets inside the heads of fish waiting to be caught and then eaten:

> They knew
> The meaning of danger, even if
> They did not know the exact recipe for dinner.

Then comes what the poet herself describes as a Gestalt shift of perspective, as she "becomes" the fish and then contemplates with placid detachment her own end:

> I am a good meal.
> In three minutes, I will cease to exist.

Through this device, the commonplace experience of eating fish in a restaurant is transformed into a meditation upon our relationship with other species and our use/misuse of the world's resources.

By way of contrast, the runner-up in this year's competition, Denise Hagan's wonderful poem 'Pietà' belongs to another tradition, that of poets writing about painting (though the term for this, ekphrasis, can also be used to cover other forms of description). Although Keats' 'Ode on a Grecian Urn' is often regarded as the classic of this kind of poetry, the 20th century boasted some fine examples too, including William Carlos Williams' 'Landscape with the Fall of Icarus' and Anne Sexton's 'The Starry Night'. 'Pietà' is a lovely addition to that tradition in which the poet movingly explores her own response to the 'granite tenderness' of Perugino's great work. And other poets in the anthology explore their own responses to visual art, for example, Michael Witts' carefully observed 'Of the Floating World', while Tom Choi in his 'Paper Crane' conjures up another kind of resurrection as art and nature combine touchingly in "a rising wish".

In the winning poem, Lina Buividaviciute's exquisite 'In November. And the clouds will gather', nature is more of a backdrop for spiritual or emotional ruminations. The poet finds herself in a slump:

> The broth is tasteless, no one chases
> the shadows out of the corners; now I think to myself
> I've been living such a lukewarm life

Nature brings no comfort, rather quite the contrary:

> The forest and the trees, the fading bedding, the winter
> berries
> and birds still not yet red, I plod down the empty
> roadsides,
> soaked in the freezing Autumn rain, the raindrops on
> my short
> eyelashes …

There is little sense of renewal here, in fact. Instead, the poet must hunker down:

> I must lean my heavy head back, get drunk with
> dampness,
> kiss the silent passer-by in the city, worship nudity,
> celebrate
> All Saints, compose a litany on hunger,
> survive this month

The poem suggests some kind of depression, beautifully, if harrowingly, evoking the kind of mental health issues that seem to have been exacerbated by the pandemic and our responses to it.

'Resurrection' by Carol Flake Chapman seems scarcely any cheerier; for although renewal in the form of spring is coming, it comes only unexpectedly, almost unwelcome:

> Why is it that each spring comes
> Like a surprise party

And her take on the mythical story of Isis piecing together Osiris' broken body, though leading to renewal, is couched in ambivalent language. Indeed, at the end of the piece, the poet skilfully lets the tape run on, as it were, leaving everything in perpetual, possibly unwelcome, motion:

as though
He had never died and as though
She will not have to do this again
And again and again and again

George Watt's 'Boy on a Boat' starts with slightly unpromising
weather—"A blue-white windy day of hard-edged clarity" and
the poet is on board the vessel to prevent the young, boisterous
passengers from

hurtling over the side
to an early and watery death

Yet from this unpromising situation, an uplifting picture
emerges: "this day is one for good will". And surely the poet
answers his own closing question:

will memory hold
the effervescence of that one bright heart

in this tender, upbeat poem.

I'd like to end by quoting the last lines of another gently
optimistic poem, 'Watching the Dusk on a Rainy Night:
Musing' by Luisa Ternau. Like other poems mentioned above,
this one touches on both nature and art, and the haunting
ending fittingly suggests the way I hope this lovely anthology
of new poetry will linger on in your memory:

A song that will not leave you
Wherever you may go
Its notes like bells
Filling the air in silence

*Jeff Streeter is a writer and critic, currently based in the UK.
He was formerly Director of the British Council in Hong
Kong.*

MESSAGE FROM
JOANNA RADWANSKA-WILLIAMS

First-prize winner
International Proverse Poetry Prize 2021

Charmed by poetry

When I look back at my life, from my earliest years I have been charmed by poetry—that mysterious rhyming force that makes words stick in memory forever.

When I was little, I was captivated by Alexander Pushkin's fairy tales. My grandmother's native language was Russian, and being an educator, she took pains to teach me that beautiful language. Pushkin's tales were so much grander than their Western counterparts—instead of Snow White and the Seven Dwarfs, there was "The Tale of the Dead Princess and the Seven Heroes". I memorised entire passages of it. My child's imagination was also stimulated by the magically beautiful illustrations of the fairy tales on little black lacquer boxes, the princess with her tresses enhanced with real gold—a Russian art form.

The Polish poetry I was exposed to as a child was quite different—full of wonder and word play. Some of the greatest national poets, such as Julian Tuwim, also contributed vastly to children's literature, or more accurately speaking, wrote poetry that transcended generations. Such is Tuwim's masterful onomatopoeic poem "The Steam Engine". Through this poem I learned how art can imitate reality, or change our perception of reality.

When I moved to England and learned English, at some point I became charmed by poets like John Keats and Gerard Manley Hopkins. I admired the denseness of their language and imagery, like the quintessence of things, like deep red wine or dark chocolate. I memorised 'Ode to Autumn' by Keats and 'God's Grandeur' by Hopkins. I learned about the mysterious creation of 'Kubla Khan' by Samuel Taylor Coleridge, with its marvellous alliterations, "Five miles meandering with a mazy motion, Through wood and dale the sacred river ran…" I wondered how Coleridge's sleeping brain could produce such things.

Later, in America, at the University of North Carolina at Chapel Hill, I took several courses in literature and in creative writing, notably from the professor of Romantic Poetry, Robert Kirkpatrick, whom I nicknamed "the eagle", because when he felt inspired when lecturing, he would flap his arms like wings, and stand on his toes, as if he were taking flight. Somehow, he unlocked that magical something in my brain, and I've made it a habit to write poetry ever since.

I am enormously grateful to Gillian and Verner Bickley for publishing my poems in the "Mingled Voices" international poetry prize anthology, and I feel so honoured to have received the first prize last year, as well as the third prize this year. It is wonderful that Proverse has created such a community of writers, that we can read and appreciate each other's poetry, and that it has been published and distributed to the world. When I was a student at Chapel Hill, I remember dreaming, together with my friends who were also taking creative writing courses, that someday our work would be anthologized. My dream has come true! May all of your beautiful dreams also come true!

Joanna Radwańska-Williams
February 2023

THE POEMS

Stroke[1]

A morning might begin like this, windows closing to light,
a punch of darkness delivered to the solar plexus of a day.

Your voice barely audible on the phone saying you'd had a fall
that you could barely move, could barely swallow.

I'll be right there. The long, tight grip of rain
on my heart. Six hours of thinking the worst before I reach.

Kind neighbours have shifted you to the hospital. You're in the
ICU, tubes and wires rudely in and out of your body.

I climb the mountain of the moment. Your eyes brighten when
they
spot me. Your gaze sews my fears. Daddy. Our hands cling.

Tomorrow I'll know a numbness colder than your skin.
A flattening of all things. How will I vocalise the rising rale of
pain?

Loss, a Peepul tree, will take roots inside my chest.
For years it will grow—leaf by leaf. For years the earth will
feel heavier.

Vinita Agrawal

Afternoon Haikus
(may be read together or disassembled)

Just outside my house
There's a busy city street.
Choose another way.

Down the path instead.
Rare to see anyone here.
Car sounds grow fainter.

City fades away.
Birds call from trees or flying by.
There are butterflies.

That leaf's atremble.
Ceylon Blue Glassy Tiger!
A quick flash then gone.

Bulbuls search the grass.
They're not looking for berries.
Grasshoppers, watch out!

Along the handrail
There's a highway for insects.
Spiders lurking too.

Cries of the Barbet
Echo through this open space
In the golden light.

I hear a White-eye
Coucal join with haunting tones
Minivets depart.

Slanting rays of sun.
As cicadas cease their sounds.
Time to head homeward.

My house is not far
But it seems a world away.
With each step - crickets!

Joy Al-Sofi

Another Overcast Day - with Occasional Heavy Showers

Every day, seems there's something
Working hard to get between me and my
Daily damp pavements,
My glimpses of the otherwise unseen.

Beyond the footpath,
Deep in the foliage
Shadows shape shift.
Leftover scraps of night
Riseon midnight wings:
Spangle Swallowtail!

Alongside the path, the rain-fed stream rushes.
Sunlight rides the rapids
Spilt milt curls on water
Like rings of smoke, or bright feathers afloat,
Heading towards an unreachable sea
Frogs bark like distant dogs.

There's a definite downturn In northward birds.
Already the drongos are flown.
I'm working on my spider census.

City girl, born and bred.
Who never imagined
Critters could matter
So much.

I've got to get out there
See who has survived the rain,
But...shower-spattered windows
Manage to restrain yet again.

Maybe tomorrow?
I can/can't wait.

Joy Al-Sofi

Gone Home

Hong Kong when I came,
was simply a backdrop of cinematic fame.
The place from where
I first saw, and fell in love
With, Lau, and Chow, and Chan.

That love's not gone, though
        dated now and faded.
The surface looks smooth, but below
        a deep current flows.

I've not been to the Bun Festival Island
Nor yet discovered Discovery Bay
I'll have to take your word
        There's migrating birds
At Mai Po, Tai Po or O.

It took quite a while,
        as the tectonics shifted
and Hong Kong changed
        Into home.

My lease here's been long
Time remaining is brief
I won't deny there's a feeling of grief.

All too soon comes
A tide that cannot be denied.
The tug is too strong
Family ties pull me along
        (and this place tu(r)ned a whole different t/one)

It's all disconcerting.
Make that downright hurting,
And where once was home
I   s gone.

Joy Al-Sofi

Leaving

Remembering as much as I can.

The waterfront shimmers sunshine and diesel
Black Kites wheel overhead
Iconic glass and steel styles.

Wondering what I will miss the most.

The MTR is one, of course.
The way it moves, the sway.
Six seats of separation
Where once was chatter-filled full
Of life and socializing.
Now all heads bow before the iPhone altar.

What will I remember the most?

Dim sum memory already dimmed
Two plus years of Covid's done that.
Cultural Centre's gone quiet too
Performing arts a thing of the past.
Jumbo is gone,
Star Ferry's close behind.

These days, I take walks outside.
Watch butterflies from concrete paths.
Nature's diminished daily,
But still holding on
For now.

It's the Hong Kong way.

Joy Al-Sofi

Once Was

Once this place was
A dazzlement
A neon Eden,
This city, this Island,
Peninsula and peak.

Extraordinary now
Only in its disilluminationment.
Once it was the buzzing heart,
The most exciting city in the world.

Neon's already long gone.
A self-inflicted
Silent take-down.

Nathan's nothing now,
But the name of another
Dimmed-down
LED-lit road
That once
Led to somewhere
You wanted to go.

Joy Al-Sofi

Passersby

Passersby pass me on pathways
Gripped in the spell of
The tiny screen.
Captured, enraptured by
Dancing digital dreams.

To these people
Nature is mute
Not even a backdrop
To an empty stage.

Not looking up.
Not looking down.
They never see or hear
Streams flowing from pebbles to bubbles
Translucent whirl-pearls
Ringing mossy rocks that slick and drip.

Real world raindrops
Jiggle on leaves like quicksilver beads.
Beneath clogged foliage
      Tiny crabs crawl.

These passersby pass
Mesmerized
As they disappear into the
Palm of their own hands.

Joy Al-Sofi

Prayer and Response

Writer's Prayer

> Let me write with texture.
> Al dente to the mind,
> Puncture readers' preconceptions.
> Lord, let my words pierce
> Like a spear in the side,
> A prick in the Moving Finger
> Dripping with blood that sizzles.

Reader's Response

> Just give me the real.
> Writers, get out of the way.
> Let life
> Come streaming in like sunlight
> Through words transparent as glass.
>
> Making me stop to admire
> Your exquisite phrases
> Doesn't move me.

It removes me.

Joy Al-Sofi

Some Things Aren't Supposed To Be Said

Some things aren't supposed to be said.
Some things just aren't
Some things…

Handmaid's Tale is fiction in France
But America's tight in the Puritan's grasp
Women's rights're a thing of the past.

Guns or kids, whichever you love
Federal laws don't unite them
It's a river of blood that does.

Priti Patel's
Sending Julian to hell
All claimed in the name of the law.

Ukraine is a shame
But Iraq was the same.
Shhhh! Not supposed to say that at all.

Some things shouldn't (ever have to) be said.

Temperatures rising
Rains out of season
Leaders' see no reason to change?

If the pied piper we follow
Is twisted and hollow
At some point,

Will we
Make it
To tomorrow?

Joy Al-Sofi

Wet Weather

Non-perennial stream
Never stopped flowing this year.
Days of no sun.
Butterflies few
Dragonflies fewer.

Giant Golden Orbweavers
Repairing damp-damaged webs
Sticky trap turns slick in rain
Tiny animated shuttles
Still young
They'll grow into their name.

Figs rot on trees
Overripe papayas unpicked
A perfect platform for insects mating
You take/get it where you can.

Lowering clouds and rising mists
Obscure the mountain yesterday revealed
From my window.

What was so clear
Mist, rain and dust
Has now disappeared
Receding like a once was memory.

There'll be different scenes
From a different facing room.
Time and distance, mist and dust
Like a curtain obscure all views.

This time next year
Will I remember this window
And a once was mountain?

Joy Al-Sofi

A wish for my old age[2]

Freedom from occupation, freedom from vanity,
Freedom from guilt, freedom from responsibility.
O, if time grants me permission to grow old,
I wish for freedoms many and manifold.

Freedom from structure, alarms, goals, lists,
Freedom to squander time as I deem fit,
Freedom from society's onerous dictates—
Be respectable, stick to the narrow and straight.

Freedom to chase every little whim and fancy,
Freedom to roll over and sleep when life gets chancy,
Throw caution to the winds, entertain thoughts unchaste,
Depart from stolid company without stealth, post-haste

Freedom to look as dowdy as you please,
Flaunt the wrinkles, let silver hair blow in the breeze,
Old age is the liberation from the tyranny of youth,
From decorum, dandyism, desires uncouth.

While freedoms many I wish to wrest from life,
To turn back time is a freedom denied,
Nor do I control the earth's gravitational pull,
That tugs at the flesh and shakes the organs loose.

When the faculties dim and memories fade,
When I rattle and hum with each exertion I make,
When the sceptre of death looms large ahead,
When time slows down, strings out life on a thread
I wish for a full heart and a comfortable bed.

Shikha Bansal

Once Again: The Courage of Everyday Life[3]

*If you can't fly then run, if you can't run then walk, if you can't
walk then crawl, but whatever you do, keep moving forward.*

    —Martin Luther King, Jr.

What're you looking at them for?
For some, a short walk is toil,
even the crawlers get to go,
but they work hard, Lord, balancing
along with every movement.
And if they carry another,
well, that is a miracle
of such complexity, Physics
there, stands aside and wonders.

Alan Bern

Out of the Blue Sea of Letters[4]

I watch my father swim edging the pearly rock
round the natural pool at Celimar, a giant oyster
shell lodging his slender mass. The water curls
and slides along the sides of his moss-green
trunks, hides and reveals his liquid loneliness,
a kingdom to which we (the fearful) are not
called. In that, his very own time, he is fish
and boat and trident god. From there his arm,
extended, guards us— upon that sight we die,
adoringly, of jealousy. What does he think of
as he swims? Nothing. He swims. He thrusts,
stretches and rests. He lets his dreams flow free,
forgets his old man's debts, impending threats
of national doom. There on that cool bed he is
a glorified body. And I— allured by sea, but
only from afar, or above (a plane), or very near
(the frothy shore). I did not learn to swim, nor
surfed through piano, just floated between idylls
and slogans. Not a wry word, maybe a sad look.
His was all deep-sea love, iridescent and blue.
One day I went to find him in that since-forsaken
beach town, Celimar. No one (but she) knew of
the lot across the park, the bike, the bar, the club-
house (—never existed, said they). Only she and
the natural pool.
    My foot is now about to tread
the jagged rock.
    A breeze distracts me, something
scurries through a beam of light. I see him emerge
from the water among these letters. He smiles,
draws close,
   splashing you,
     and invites you to read me.

Maria Elena Blanco

I Dreamt I Was on The Yangtze River[5]

Also called Chang Jiang
the longest river in all of Asia
full of eternal living history
water being ageless and all of that.

I dreamt one night
I was in a boat heading steadily upstream
throughout all of China.

Rising at Jari Hillin the Tanggula Mountains
6'300 kilometres long
it flows all the way
into the East China Sea.

A vital part
of the Chinese Economy
I read
since the Han Dynasty.

The irrigation system
built in 256 BC
during the warring states period
built by the kingdom of Quin
still in use today
providing stable farming
for all of beautiful China.
I don't know why I dreamt about it
as I was never there in my life.

Gavin Bourke

My Rare Chinese Winding-Clock[6]

A black rectangular box, missing hands, missing the pendulum
with a silver dial with three red number fives imprinted on it, in
the inner circle
and emblazoned with the words 'Made in Shanghai'.
I bought it in a market on the southside of Dublin one Saturday
Morning
for about ten euros, a fair price considering its very poor
condition.
For a long time, I imagined it complete such was my
fascination and imagination
I thought of swirling oriental artwork and intricate decorative
carvings.
So, one day I googled it and found the complete clock
the essence I had purchased was enough to correctly identify it
properly
and it was more beautiful than I had ever imagined.
Made by hand in the nineteen-fifties with black metal hands
the shiniest silver pendulum hanging from the movement
enclosed in a hand-painted glass case of ornate Chinese floral
designs
with five gorgeous finials and embossed with brass mouldings
or carvings
of snakes or dragons intertwined on the pieces affixed to the
wooden-box core.
The works completely brass and still intact in my clock
I intend to finish the pictures in reality
and order the wooden and mechanical components
so that my cherished clock
will one day be restored to its former glory.
How little I knew when I bought it that day, covered in old
paint on a stone floor
but the dial caught my eye and intrigued me, my mind doing
somersaults at first sight.
What did the Chinese lettering mean?
Why was there, three red number five numerals in a triangular
shape on the dial?

it was a horological mystery
I intended to solve
and I knew
I had the resolve to do so.

Gavin Bourke

Any Thing[7]

The strap hung loose and the watch
tightened on the wrist;

it was two stories
one from the corner of each eye, housewares sinking
in a pool and a bed, new people in my space
leaving for work through the noisy door that nicks
your knuckles when you unlock it. The lock,
too, sinking rapidly in the pool. I follow the souls
up Twenty-First Street, subway, sinking
with trotting heads, all with wet hair.
The other an elegant garden of bedside tools:
clock, book, antacid, glass, and remote
against blue, a leg, then a falling woman's
body, then a man's, eyes on each other
or closed. Subway crashing me from thought,
breath ending where anything looks beautiful.

Lawrence Bridges

A Letter to My Child of War

Oh child of mine, they say, when boys are born
for the whole generation— the war is upon us.
We birthed our sons around that time—we rejoiced, matriarchs
of the family,
but dark shapes loomed, there was no peace. My grandmother
had
already seen those shapes, before the Second World War, she
saw the sign of the cross
in the sky, women, solitudinous, hauling on their shoulders all
the yokes
of the world. On September 11you'll turn eighteen, so I keep
anxiously
glancing at the sky, following the news from neighboring
lands.

And yet I forgive you for being born, the child of war.

I can't begin to tell you, how much I wish never to mark in
lamb's blood
the door of our home upon your return. I fervently hope you'll
never know,
how much it weighs down my hands and heart,
the chill of the steel, when sweat breaks out
on sleepless nights as I count those fallen. Is this hope meant
for you, or for me?

Still, what frightens the most aren't the stumps,
the phantoms of limbs, or the hair that's gone white—

but to never escape
the barren wind ghosts, and that nothing will be
as it was.

And yet I let you go, my child of war—
my reins can't hold back the steeds any longer.

Lina Buividaviciute

About the Legs

I likely stepped into the world on the wrong foot.
I still don't know which foot
is the right one, I still don't know
if there is a right one—

what do I know what do I know what do I
know— one somehow becomes
a woman with a downturned
mouth, with a Shar Pei face,
a woman with the sparkle no longer effervescent
in her eyes, with faulty inner
thermometers, a lukewarm woman,
with loneliness dripping out of her bag—

one somehow becomes a sad-faced woman—
a she-spirit who's left her tribe, a sister who sold
Josephs, with nuphars of sorrow entangled
in her hair, a woman who writes about the dark
ages, the blackest of nights, and little daughters not being
born—-

So what do I know what do I know what do I know—
I do not know on which foot I'll step out of this world.

Lina Buividaviciute

In November. And the clouds will gather

The world, deep in sleep, a window and an overcast
glance, there's no one to wake me up, the darkness slowly
engulfs the light of day, it's difficult to discern what
time it is, everything recedes somehow: the fog, the window
pane,
I need stronger glasses, increasingly expressive rituals.

I don't want to get up in the morning, I growl and build tents
from bedsheets like a child; it is but an echo, I can't rekindle
the joyful game. The broth is tasteless, no one chases
the shadows out of the corners; now I think to myself
I've been living such a lukewarm life, it's not even November
yet.

The forest and the trees, the fading bedding, the winter berries
and birds still not yet red, I plod down the empty roadsides,
soaked in the freezing Autumn rain, the raindrops on my short
eyelashes ——

I try to repeat, to answer aloud, I hoot my laughter
at the entrance of the hall of death, having to rebuild my
vitality from ashes,
I need blood and milk, but my veins are barren.

I must lean my heavy head back, get drunk with dampness,
kiss the silent passer-by in the city, worship nudity, celebrate
All Saints, compose a litany on hunger,
survive this month.

Lina Buividaviciute
Translated by Irma Šlekytė

Potiphar's Wife

*After a time, his master's wife looked at Joseph with longing
and said, "Lie with me."* The Bible, the Book of Genesis

I cling onto Your robe, boldly tear the seams apart,
rip up my pride to pieces with my teeth,
though You arrived at our home a slave.
You said You're acting in his name, the one who never
abandons,
gives strength to resist the forbidden bodily orifices.
My desire entangles my veins, the thin blood
mixes with the thick, the red and the blue—
nothing matters any more, I rub away the imprint
of the ring. I'm a young gazelle, awaiting the nimblest
of the herd. I always get what I crave for, in this abode
with curtains of the most precious purple
even the flicker of the flame abides by me.
Never hide behind his name, the ninth commandment—
I'm just a wilting fussy mimosa, who's never been
rejected before, not even out of fear. You played
the most sensitive strings without ever touching the zither of
my body.
I cling onto Your robe, I'm a she-wolf in heat, I tear
apart my loneliness, my boredom, my slow decline, I bite
at Your righteous heart, I devour Your liver. We'll rot
in the cells of our pride, our bones will never rest together.

Everything I betray to the crowd afterwards will be out of
despair.

Lina Buividaviciute

The Foam of the Days[8]
Inspired by Boris Vian's novel *Froth on the Daydream*

Unfamiliar greenery entangles my feet
I can't breathe in— the flowers of oddness bloom there,
resin-smelling racemes— I breathe the smoke in and out,
I'm a small dragon, a stranger to my own tribe.

I'm a lover afflicted with the sickness of being an outsider,
In a small garden, I drink Chinese tea from a yellow
china set, and no one knows that is where I
cough up my unusual symptoms, all of the
abnormality.

Sometimes, late in the evening, you visit me,
when no one sees how you creep alongside
the thick hedges of my hair, the cracking porcelain of my
skin—
you're afraid to be too traditional, too predictable, afraid
that the readings of your internal thermometers will reach
extreme cold—

it's convenient for you to smear yourself with my sickness, my
seclusion,
so that you can surprise others with spectacular storms,
so that they applaud this peculiar art— but having not fallen ill,

you will grow a creeper in your lungs that move like bellows—
and the normal ones no longer lack for anything— so that
I do not infect them with decay, so that I don't sow the seeds of
frailty in their healthy fields.

Lina Buividaviciute

The Shining
Inspired by Stephen King's novel *The Shining*

What will you find in the memory cutouts, Daddy?
How will you explain the black dream mutations,
the degenerated hedge beasts?

It was all inside of us from the beginning, we always
needed a reliable light to see within— long dog trails
of history, bulging veins of the house—
I remember it all, that's why at night my dark
earthen brother is calling me—

Can you hear the loud thumping of hooves, Daddy?
These walls are too thin, you're already breathing so heavily—
my time bone is still open, my fear nerve still exposed.

I soar in your Purgatory, I'm a lost little boy,
they say I was the Sunday child, I had six feelings,
but the hammer's so hard, it beats rhythmically, forcefully—

the thunder is rumbling with fury, Daddy,
it's raging against our windows—
so what's the use of shining so desperately?

Lina Buividaviciute

Five photos of Diana[9]

I wait each day in hope to see at night
some piece, a part of you I've yet to see
I wait to look again in dark half-light

I wait I search each one and hope to find
in some moment a girl a world away
I wait to glean fragments I can combine

I wait, distil a drop, a drip each time
slowly decant each night a spirit fire
I wait to then imbibe this dream sublime

Sean Camshon

Resurrection[10]

Why is it that each spring comes
Like a surprise party even though
We should have been expecting it
And we have been looking for gifts
Hidden away inside bare branches
And packages deep within the earth
Already beginning to rise and open
As Isis begins to gather the pieces
Of the lost and fallen and riven god
We had given up on and artfully
Puts them together as though
He had never died and as though
She will not have to do this again
And again and again and again

Carol Flake Chapman

Paper Crane[11]

Sarah focused on the standard square:
Began some thick and raspy account to unfold,
Treacheries, atrocities, the like by human hands.

When she saw it, when she saw a bird of grace
Resurrected, she had only a rising wish.
This paper crane can be any colour.

To you, this paper crane, I wish, would carry love.

Tom Choi

Railway Station When the Doors Open[12]

Next station, Sheung Wan.
From Monday to Friday I see a picture,
A peak hour tidal movement
In the station when the doors open.

Cell phones, big ads, men and women…
By heart I follow. I stand and play a part.
Every weekday I see the picture,
The movement when the doors open.

I hesitate, observe,
And calculate my steps.
          Out of the train
We move among ourselves…
Black hair, gray hair, a few hundred faces.
          Forward. Exit.
Some in a hurry, others not too much.
Saint Laurent and Burch
Line up for a lift.
The heavy-footed
Outpace the escalator.
You take the lead. I maintain my steps.
Eight-thirty, we move at different paces
In the station when the doors open.

You may recall "La Prospérité", the picture's name,
When there is room about enough
For the men and women to move among themselves.
          And the painter?

Tom Choi

Full Moon In Another Country

The moon has followed us here,
though we have learnt already
its secrets of darkness and renewal,
of waning and growing to fullness again.

How beautiful you look in its pale light,
the worries faded from your eyes,
the scars of terror beginning to disappear.

Tomorrow in our new rooms
we will hang the paintings we rolled for the journey,
refusing to leave everything we loved behind.

William Leo Coakley

Music In The Air
for Nadir Aslam and Kristin Olson

Saved by the surgeon's knife,
I lie on my bed alone,
Half remembering who I am,
Never forgetting the pain.

Suddenly into my room
Whirls of Vivaldian joy
Pull me back from the gloom,
Lift me into the day.

I can hear life calling
"Nothing more to fear,"
Its message of healing:
Music in the air.

William Leo Coakley

Haven Among Trees[13]

stroll among lofty woodland friends,
shelter us from searing sun, pelting rain
providers of houses and food
for raccoons,gray squirrels, wood ducks

my fingertips trace the bark of a bitternut hickory
vertical ridges with holes bored by hungry
beetles and red-bellied woodpeckers

I place one ear to your aging trunk
listen and hope for a conversation;
too many times, your stressful
gurgles, clicks have gone unheard

a wood thrush sings chk-chk-chk,
ra-vi-o-li, ee-oh-lay,
fweet-fweet-fweet

complements my mantra
of om śāntih śāntih śāntih-
peace, peace, peace

my pulse slows, breaths deepen
mind harnesses thoughts of
obligations, debts, illness

woods nurture and awaken
my conscience to act and respond
to your distress calls and to mine
in the hope of saving each other

Suzanne Cottrell

Body Full of Heatstroke[14]

A brand-new desierto was found traveling
cross-country TSA agents are tapping out
when desierto comes through the x-ray machine.

Notice the healthy hipbone and femurs
ingrained in the copper sand, glittering.

Desierto, grown, was spotted at a rooftop party.
Mid-dance storm and helpless, his skin
trembled at the bass, shoulders popped

through the oasis of his mouth, Tito dove in.
He burned hotter than clayware in kiln; sand
steeped, he grew closer to a bronze sunset.

To our surprise, yes, desierto was blown
up by Tito. His dune body was left leaking
steam all over blurring the dance floor.

It caused everyone to dream big, and good
men came to live in this sandcastle moment.

Gayly, desierto became human and a good
metaphor for sweat. For bones. For spread
eagle. A good metaphor pa' lo santitos glad
at the impromptu wake; the party held him

as he is, desiertito attended his wake bare body
only in bright yellow briefs; mira sol peered
in the windows and blinds streaked him, son.

Julio Diaz

7 miles high,
Ivory Coast, western Africa, 29th November 1973.[15]

                  The remains removed from the jet's engine
         consist of feathers: five complete and fifteen partial,

                         found from wings,
         (secondaries, lesser and underwing coverts)

                         tail, neck and breast,
        which, aligned with comparative material

                         in the U.S.
      National Museum of Natural History,
                    allow certain identification

                         as Rüppell's Griffon

       thereby confirming this endangered vulture holds
            the altitude record for a bird in flight.

      Did you leave this scavenged earth to fly for the sun?

                               Neil Douglas

A found poem:

Laybourne, Roxie C (December 1974) "Collision between a Vulture and an Aircraft at an altitude of 37,000 feet." *The Wilson Bulletin*.86 (4):461-462.

Bruce Lee in a yellow tracksuit[16]

is listening to the grass grow,
        thinking he will be immune against suffering.

But he says the act of thought is suffering
        so he tells us we should instead be feeling

because if we are in the moment, feeling,
        we are not distracted by the finger

pointing to the sky. He tells us to look beyond the finger,
        feel the tender glory of the moon,

the heavenly bodies that complement the moon –
        what compels the night to shine – the dog stars, our
sun.

All that grows on Earth is because of our sun
        and what springs from the earth can be beautiful.

A single blade of grass tells us life is beautiful.
        Bruce Lee in a yellow tracksuit is listening to the grass
grow.

Neil Douglas

Geography Teacher[17]

He is the sign at Land's End
Pointing to John O' Groats

His fields were mixed and arable
Barley, sheep, and oats

Then an oxbow lake adrift
From apathetic silt

Now a rock-strewn summit
Eroded by fast glacial melt

His life's contours closely packed
Signify the climb as steep

Above the tor the trees are sparse
The ravine below is deep

Neil Douglas

Mr Milano[18]

such a charming man
perfect English with a balsamic accent
lapsing on occasion to native Tuscan
andiamo a ballare
spoken through a jeopardy of crowded teeth
commuters on a platform waiting for his smile to slide open

*

he asked me up for coffee and biscotti
at his tiny flat with a river view
to discuss how his heart had beat at random
since chancing by her at the Rivoli
how her skin tasted of vinegar
how he had left his hope at her door

*

such a charming man he told me how
he removed the dust jackets of other afternoon women
ran his spindle fingers down their spines
turned their once cream pages to parchment
could have been a professor
could have been a gigolo
such well-manicured cuticles this charming man

*

si balla
her rhythm for his *libretto*
her hand cupped on his boney shoulder
his hand pressed into the bow curve of her back
pressed hard into the curve
bene ora si balla
her hand clasped to his
her body fast to his
her hips' insistent sway
to the random beat of his heart
the random gasp of his heart
the rent of his heart
this man this charming man

Neil Douglas

Blanchot

I didn't know
Back in 2008
That one day I will be arrested
By the memory of her
Discussing Blanchot,
Whom I never cared to teach.
How did that image from the past
Catch up with me?
The boring conference,
The intellectual circus
At The Westin Long Beach—

Four days of quest in the ultimate West,
Yet, on the third,
We had to sneak out;
The beautiful philosophy PhD
Bewitched me— still a candidate
Back than at HKU's Complit.
We took the train to Los Angeles
Just to see
The HOLLYWOOD sign on Mount Lee
And witness the decadence
Of the Avenue of the Stars.

Back to The Westin at night,
To make sure the egotistic show
Was over, but then Blanchot
Made an entrée,
Son of a b …, and he
Made her dive too deep in philosophie
Française
That turned red wine into café au lait,
Just beside the bed
But not on it,
Till the rooster crowed at dawn.

It wasn't how I planned my trip
To the US of A—
The end of the world.

I don't understand though
Why it still feels so painful
To remember and think
How I had to depart with Blanchot
And return to Hong Kong—
O, responsabilité!

Ahmed Elbeshlawy

Sandy Eyes

I was just waiting for my mother
To pick me up after school,
Looking at nothing, thinking about nothing
But her arrival, when particles of sand
Flew out of this boy's hand
Like tiny bullets to fill my eyes,
Inflaming and blinding them for a few
But unusually long minutes.
There was no reason for that.

Years later, I was just trying to understand
The world through reading literature,
When those eyes with the colour of the sand
Blinded me again— this time,
For unusually long years to come.
There was no reason for that either.

Now, it is the memory of the sandy eyes—
Mine and yours— that dictates these lines
With a passion and a pain streaming through.
Sandy Eyes— the eyes still haunting me—
You might be surprised to know,
That the one thing I ever wanted to do
Is to see my eyes looking at you.

Ahmed Elbeshlawy

Sinai

In the desert of Sinai,
The stars seemed to be closer.
The cold night, though quiet,
Had the loudest voice.
The mountains made me feel
Insignificant.

The Bedouins smoked
Like there was no tomorrow.
European tourists sat around the fire,
Listening to my stories with
Sleepless eyes spelling desire—
For the sand spoke of horses and blood
And deities made of mud
That drove numberless armies through the desert
With an eye on beautiful Kemet.

I used to think of one thing; how to bring
The stars down to earth.
They "do not give a damn", as Auden said,
Yet, they did look down upon me that night
And assured me that one day I will write
About them from a foreign land,
When they become one with the one
Who broke my heart, back in Cairo,
And released the ceaseless ink of this pen.

Ahmed Elbeshlawy

The Onslaught of Sameness

"And there came dreadful sameness
My long-lost lonely lover.
I'm sorry it took me some
Time to write you this letter.

Let me say that I never
Doubted your heart or your love;
I never imagined that
Anyone would love me more,
But, by the time your muse came
To understand the meaning
Of your young uniqueness,
The depth of penetration
That accompanies your name,
Everything became the same.

People's faces mingled and
Became one big listless face,
The trees around our old place
That we named one by one in
Our dreamy youth became
Just local flora to my
Deteriorated eyesight.
The cats, somehow, lost their grace;
They obeyed now without shame.
The warm seasons lost passion,
And the winter lost its bite.

The "dog from hell" that you kept
Making up in your poems
To chase you all of your life
Didn't seem to be any
Different from the stray dogs the
Authorities killed around
This place every other night.

Yes, I have been thinking of
The loving look in their eyes—
Those dogs that resembled you—

And I did cry once or twice
When I remembered their barks—
And your words and your poems—
The rattling of chains inside
The van of the dog police;
The rattling of chains inside
Your wounded masochist heart—
That dog that you crucified
At my dead-end street and my
Small untouchable garden—
Untouchable just to you,
Simply because you were and
Still are too much to handle.

When sameness finally came,
It made my days, my nights, my
Cigarettes, my body parts
And everything all the same.
It is now for this reason
All my parts are united
In the thought that your dear love
Must remain unrequited".

Ahmed Elbeshlawy

renewal

when I am one hundred, inclusive language will be rain and
bulb
        and we shall use these to plant and harvest and nourish
when I am one hundred, skin colour will be as autumn leaves
        and the viewfinders of *we* Phones shall frame wonder
and awe
when I am one hundred, the animals of the earth will be holy of
holies
        and they shall no longer know the bullet, the knife and
the net
when I am one hundred, senator trees will be left their roots
        just as the elderly shall know deference and reverence
when I am one hundred, charity and kindness will be
monetized
        and the currency of billionaires shall be free hospitals
and schools
when I am one hundred, the atmosphere will be rich with
oxygen
        and we shall only hear of fossil fuel deployment in war
museums
when I am one hundred, every household will care for a dog or
a cat
        and everyone shall know what it is to love thy
neighbour as thyself
when I am one hundred, social media will be as the solar
system
        and we shall not see dark matter but for the billions of
stars
when I am one hundred, games will have no scorekeeper nor
outcome
        and everyone shall know the thrill of competition and
the joy of play
when I am one hundred, the stock exchange will stock things
useful
        and those who visit shall not want for food, shelter or
friends
when I am one hundred, the gender rainbow will be the vault of
heaven

and this shall be the flag of Yahweh and of all nations
and peoples
when I am one hundred, *climate change* will be axis, tilt and
rotation
        and we shall only seriously discuss the *Four Seasons*
of Vivaldi
when I am one hundred, poetry will be printed on cereal boxes
        and the most important meal shall be metaphor and
granola
when I am one hundred, children will sit with lawmakers and
politicians
        and adults shall navigate legislation with moral
compasses
when I am one hundred, houses of worship will only honor *one
visit*
        and the faithful shall have as many homes as they do
houses
when I am one hundred, the statues of despots will populate
town squares
        and only flying and roosting birds shall prove interest
of duty
when I am one hundred, heads of state will be first among foot
soldiers
        and they shall use feet to run opposite of war and no
heads will roll
when I am one hundred, jails and courts will house ghouls and
ghosts
        and we shall visit on Hallowe'en to recall the horrors
of jurisprudence
when I am one hundred, indigenous peoples will have
reclaimed their land
        and generations of colonizers shall exchange loot bags
for tourist visas
and when I am one hundred, I and my partner will make love
like acrobats
        and we shall give thanks for middle age and our next
hundred years

Dean Gessie

bringer of light

do you stop
 when there is no use
or do you choose to rise up

I think my heart still hurts
 but I have not allowed myself
 any space
 to watch
         do I break away then
  from
  skin from
  flesh
  like a tattoo ripped apart

where do you go
         if   forever
if water says its name
especially when it listens
 especially when
 especially if you
 are afraid

 do you see that
at the opening of the light
bad people whose plan
 created this hold of life

  what angry girl do we thank for then
for the light
she now brings us

Olga Gonzalez Latapi

Or So Says the Wind

I suspect there are bears that dream too, long
to become a deconstruction of teeth and hide
just bones beneath the earth. There remains

an inability in being, to emerge into hereness
while others fail to recognize distance between
yesterday and tomorrow. An acceptance

past unattended burials of the slumbering
bears left in the soil. We must discover
a way out of such torpor, those close dens

hollow comfort to hidden giants, now
dismissed like myths or intimacies, hush
the only sound when there's no one out there.

Casey Hampton

Sarah Van Fleet Come Dawn[19]

Morning dew glistens
A flower becomes
Quivering silent

Crenulated petals pink
Crowning the unfurling bloom
Pearls held by soft spider silk

Raindrops sweet in fall
Open mouths to sing
Round songs of release

Casey Hampton

Trees

When the limb of the tree breaks
crashing to the earth
we miss its musical rush
so enamoured is the ear in the sudden crack:
Stillness split open at its seams by vacancy
jolted birds lift in flight on instinct alone,

the trunk does not weep or mourn such absence,
no words for whole or repair
only another way to frame galaxies.

Casey Hampton

Imagine Nation[20]

It's not always certain that I'm asleep or awake.
Sometimes I can be both.
The worst dreams are the ones
Where everything's going brilliantly … and yet,
There's a tiny part of you that knows you're dreaming.
Watching you, judging you, pitying you.
That's my dream.

Once again,
I find myself wearing shapeless clothes
And staring out of broken windows
For long periods,
Like a Victorian ghost.
I have no idea if this means I'm depressed,
Or just a Victorian ghost?
Perhaps I'm both?

I have heightened awareness … and yet,
I am unfamiliar in my safe space.
Temporarily dis-
connected
From the thin sliver of rationality
That glues me together.
My mind is a locked vault.
And I have lost the key.

Time, my old adversary,
is exacting its revenge.
Recent events happened to somebody else
Long ago.
This morning I gave a silent scream
Discovering the label that had been
Scratching away at my back for weeks
was actually a cornflake.

I am losing my grip on a suspended reality
That already felt tenuous and shaky.
I feel the world and everyone in it
Melting away like wax figurines.

I am in a dream
Everything else is hyper-real.
Colours are too bright,
Sounds too loud,
People too close.
Huge clown-like people with sad faces
Under their cartoon masks.

I am tormented by the persistent feeling
Nothing and no-one around me is real.
Or that I'm trapped behind glass,
Sleeping Beauty's tomb.
I make sound,
But it's muffled.
I create pictures,
But I can't see past the glare.
I doubt everything,
Including my own existence.
I am perennially preoccupied fact-checking I exist.

My psychiatrist also seems perennially preoccupied fact-
checking I exist.

'Do you know why you're here?'
'I came in for a mortgage and some baked beans.'

The disapproving grandfather clock
That tuts away the time speeds up.
Then stops.
I float on a beam of dust to the ceiling fan
And see myself gesticulating madly.
Like a sign language interpreter,
Only much more uncomfortable.
Like a sign language interpreter
in a porn film.

I need to focus.
Dial down the potently persuasive prattle
Of my polluted, pestilent, permanently 'on'
Internal monologue.
But the racing thoughts

Competing for my attention
Just set up house and proliferate.
Using my mind as a factory,
Establishing their abusive powerbase,
Harnessing my memory's
Supernatural resources,
Stamping out counterfeit copies,
Choking out my darkest fears,
Gasping my desires,
Twisting me into a seditious science fiction.

My imagination is shrinking me,
Making me subhuman.
I can't breathe.
So, I slip on my mask and slip out for a run.
The streets of Sai Kung are eerily hushed.
I start to feel a little self-conscious.
A scrum of black kites huddle in a banyan.
I wouldn't say I'm paranoid,
But they look to me like they're planning a coup.

Hong Kong shimmers and spins,
But its atoms do not hold together.
They are too bright, immaterial,
And shaking like flip-book cartoons.
I don't feel real either.
My pale skin looks garish
And it panics me to feel the thought,
'Move your hand' echo cavernously
And then see my hand move in
Slooooow-moooootion.
The whole process is supposed to be
Instant, automatic. Untraceable.

My brain is my own worst enemy,
Conducting this orchestral madness.
I melt. I tingle. I go numb.
Lose feeling in my fingers
And in my bitten tongue.
My mind is a conduit of chaos,
Of broken logic and eerier realms.

I am wrestling with illusion,
Fighting with ghosts,
Being defeated by insane delusion.

My thoughts race, swerve
And fracture into rivulets.
Many opposing realities
Are happening at once.
My head is a tornado,
Blurred by emotion
That changes so
Fast and furiously,
Splitting me open,
Like a juicy watermelon.

My skull feels too tight
And my hair hurts.
My hands are frozen into claws.
My memories lack vitality.
I'm not even convinced
They are my memories.
I feel a voyeur in my own life.
I see myself seeing out of my own eyes.
I hear myself talking to my own brain.

'Do you know why you're here?'
'Do you?'

It occurs to me
The most unreliable witness
In my own life
Is me.

Sadie Kaye

Tidal Slave[21]

The bipolar sea hypnotizes me
—Lying flat one minute,
Attention-seeking the next.
Like my imagination,
it is too vast, too powerful,
too unrestrained and unfathomable.
I am drawn to it and repelled by it.
My mother drowned in it.
I can never trust it.
Yet, I like how it mirrors my moods.
Like the sea, I am raging against the tide,
While locked into its repetitive cycle.

Hong Kong was once a thief
who stole from the sea
—tipped rubbish in it, then built on it.
But you cannot cheat the sea.
Locked in bitter pursuit,
The sea returned to reclaim the stolen land,
Swallowing Kowloon, the New Territories
and the outlying islands whole as payback;
flicking a lascivious tongue
at the neon beanstalks that had grown defiantly high;
devouring giants on billboards,
choking on diesel trucks,
belching bridges, spitting up bodies.

The sea is becoming bolder,
inspired by my impetuousness.
Angry rolling waves,
whipped into a frenzy
by my electricity,
thrash the shore with spray.
I twirl in a tumult of stormy air.
But my anguished words are blurred
by the buccaneering brutality
of the next wave that hits me.

My life, real and imagined,
flashes before my eyes.
I know I am drowning,
even before my mermother
swims towards me and sighs,
'You cannot cheat the sea.'
I smile back ruefully.
Our cyclothymic energy,
always so closely aligned.
The sea has returned to reclaim me.

I wait for the sea to respond to me in wild fury.
But it is a calm and listless vault of silver,
like a sheet of looking glass,
mocking my inner turmoil.
Even the sea has abandoned me.

Sadie Kaye

youth's decadence[22]

cured by bitter fruit, I feigned gratitude
for the inner truth revealed had not yet been ordained
by familiar soothsayers
and thus, its lessons remained in the gateway waiting to be
properly received
by the Gods I entertained, their power I long ago had deemed
absolute
I cowered in delight; their vigour refused to be contained in
spite of better reason

to this house of ruin, no matter the distance my flight took me,
I remained a slave
I laboured against bone-crushing conceit that I was someone
who mattered,
the solid ground beneath my feet was whittled away by felling
pickax and round-nosed shovel
little by little, day by day I dug my grave

I had journeyed to the city in search of a job.
When I returned, I had received no letter, no spam mail;
the post office informed me there had been no one there for
over a week.
I told them this was no longer my place of residence rather my
ill-fated tomb

lock me inside, the lord of the flies will find me, I declared,
listless and bored of the opportunities provided for me
I denied monetary substance
that sort of existence didn't seem to suit me
naked and unprotected, I felt life still eluded me.
I sacrificed creature comforts for art, I made out with dazzling
lights
spun from the wheel of chance, black or red, odd or even; when
I lost when I won more frequent
I became a monster no one who had known me could recognize
I was a carpet clown with no audience to amuse
I danced alone.

Zachary Knox

Forty-One

It took one year to
figure out that some things
had reverted to zero. It took
one year to learn that—
one year of indifference to my
silence on instant messaging
to learn that all love affairs
start at zero, with
the formalities.
I thought that
it was just a number
until I found out that
it mattered a lot more to them
and that they had projected
their fear onto me.
Now I am
my new self,
backstopped at forty
and nowhere to head
but forward, beaten
and erased.

Gary Lai

A Good Day[23]

A boy who's aged eleven
Wakes up from broken dreams.
He reaches his old cellphone
And shoots today's routine.

He sets his camera tripod
And films himself in bed.
He pulls away his blanket,
"Hello, my friends," he said.

And still without a T-shirt,
He holds a selfie stick.
He speaks and spins and sniggers,
And staggers like a chick.

His breakfast treats him quite well—
The milk is not expired.
His television's turned on.
But he is not inspired.

The screen tells awful stories—
The Earth laments in pain:
The plague is far from over;
Our new wound's in Ukraine.

The boy explains the world news.
He comments on his school.
He sings high like a diva
And dances like a fool.

He stops his cam the moment
He finds he's done a lot.
A bath is what he needs most—
It should be nice and hot.

He traps himself in bubbles.
They look like crystal balls.
Quite soon the water gets cold
As Mother seems to call.

The boy gets out to see her
And finds himself alone.
What cuddles him's a towel.
No one else is home.

He gets back to the video that
Would bring his dad a smirk.
He knows there's Wi-Fi up there—
His dad can see his work.

The clock forgets to tell him
It's nearly six fifteen.
He skips his lunch completely,
His stomach starts to scream.

But nothing's gonna stop him
From editing his clip.
He wants a cool conclusion
To make his film a hit.

His eyes begin to turn red
As he completes the end.
He speaks about his parents,
His grandma and his friends.

The time is now eleven,
He climbs to bed for dreams.
He turns off his old cellphone,
And ends today's routine.

But what he doesn't notice
Is that his Mum returns.
She's not been back for two days—
The ill are her concern.

She cleans herself and walks in
To see her boy asleep.
She kisses him and covers
His bare back and his feet.

The day is grey and simple.
He may be feeling down.
Yet millions lose their everything;
The lad's still safe and sound.

Ho Cheung Lee

Machu Picchu[24]

Yet another request from me to get the large screen fixed. The IT master was helpful enough to get things rewired and I was told this morning the classroom was ready for all the technological magic to happen. So, I went regally in with my almighty black device like how Moses came down from Mount Sinai with his stone tablets, ready to enlighten.

> it all goes dim
> for the sparkles to become fire
> those shushes

Testing. It went flawless with the first clip played with penetrating sounds. Yet, the real deal was the travel video I intended to use. The one I spent a week editing and putting the music together as if this were to be sent out for the Oscars. It was all for the remembrance of the days when we could meet faces, not masks. Germany was an era of peace and harmony, but the circling loading sign provided a perfect anticlimax. All twenty-four children watched the show of nothingness in awkward silence while I was trying to find the staff to split the ocean.

> pretentious tuning
> conductor asks for random notes
> to shroud himself

There was no turning back. I was determined to see the sunrise even knowing it would not pierce through the clouds this morning. I un-mirrored my screen, played the video, and mirrored again to reach a partial success. Just that the sound didn't go right. Things turned into whispers and concealed music. The aura of romance watered down into a low-budget listening assignment. Did anyone mention that Moses tripped over his own tablets? When I came to think of it, *Wi-Fi* did sound like a question and I was consistently convinced that *technology* contains *gone* rather than *new*.

the stone walls
of Machu Picchu stand firmly
gapless like water

Ho Cheung Lee

Moonlight[25]

I bought some money today
and they only accepted cash.

Left office early, I travelled to Mong Kok
by train, feeling I'd be less traceable.

From a metropolitan to a slum, this mall failed
to set up my virgin visit. She saw me once I

stepped in (naked, her face. Lunchtime switched
her back to herself) and asked what I was looking for.

Mercantile Bank, a one hundred dollar note,
1974, I said. She took one from the display cabinet,

wrapped in its plastic shroud.
Graded 58— it was supposed to mean a visible

fold across the note. But, wait, it was mint.
She talked about all sorts of things,

from moisture absorbers to the Queen's advancing years.
Ngo— I flinched at the foul pitch of an old man's

intrusive singing. Vest and sandals. He
turned out to be the one running the shop.

The short tryst ended with me bringing
home a crimson trophy. I slid it cautiously

out of the envelope. Time was frozen in its
translucent capsule. I caressed its sleek face,

imagining the texture, only to discover a tiny
ink mark. Top left corner, under which

a pair of fang bites sat there like a staple
punched into my eye. 20 times its face value now,

I toyed it like a pinhole camera against
my dining room light. Looking through

the larger opening, a stream of grey light emerged,
unveiling a murky, melancholy, misshapen moon.

Ho Cheung Lee

Replay[26]

Last night before bedtime I went through
the WhatsApp group chats as if
I were to prepare for a test tomorrow.

Aunts and uncles were sending names
for Big Uncle to order wreaths.
What a custom we Chinese
have— messages with names of the senders
to go with the pale flowers.

Tens of lines to scroll up before
the weeping emojis.
Aunt Lillian said she was rushing to
the airport only to learn in twenty minutes
that his journey was over.

Fingertip swept downward, numbers
descended, some 60, 70, 120.
Pictures of monitors displaying wavy
lines and colourful figures like in the stock market.
People wearing masks. White bedding.
Dim light.

There was a series of congrats notes
for Cousin Wang's Master's Degree
before I reached the last video of Grandpa,
in his chequered pyjamas,
slowly picking up his fish ball noodles at home.
His chopsticks stuffed him a mouthful
and he bit off the excess before chewing.

Ninety-eight years in eighteen seconds.

Ho Cheung Lee

A Birthday Meditation

Now I approach
that fearsome age
when all is pared to lean;
when gold and glories count
for naught,
and no exertions can divert
mortality's unblinking gaze.

This body is both me
and not,
a mere yet wondrous tool;
it filters all perception,
is indeed the intersection
of my inner self with
all that is without.

But who is it—
this "self", this "I",
this spirit, mind or soul,
this ever-changing constant
that, from birth to now, still
somehow
remains me?

Does it endure beyond this life
within another realm,
a parallel existence,
a dimension yet unknown?
Or do I simply vanish—
poof!
into the mystery?

Sharon Ludan

And the Universe Responds[27]
(Sequel to, 'To the Universe', *Mingled Voices 5*)

So, poet, you ask what more I want of you;
well, I could ask the same
of you— already blessed
with sturdy body,
hearty health
to thrive several decades;
true love and deep;
precious children to replenish your heart's joy;
a curious mind, sharp, clear
and quick; work full and fun,
to stretch every skill, grow your best power;
dreams in abundance: aim, set and go…
Beauty! you must have it,
seize and express it, imbibe
and absorb it,
make it your own.

Now you come wailing,
What's left to be done,
is life all behind me,
what's next for me now?

Well, don't expect answers
from me at this point.
(You know me by now.)
Exquisite mystery is still my constant.
Shall I banish you to a tropical isle;
isolate you in a global pandemic;
appall you with political maelstrom?
None of these strike to your deepest fears…

Look to yourself, as always you must
still be brave,
to the very end.
Blessings, beauties, gifts bestowed—
how will you use them?

This I ask of you, and more.

Sharon Ludan

A wasteland of arrows[28]

Fill the sky with your piped updreams and destitute opinions.
Mockery comes in the form of insults masked as compliments.

Potato peelers are used to tear layers of skin from your
osteoporosis inflicted bones; hang them on bamboo poles like
dirty laundry.

Have a side of jam with that toxic blood pudding dipped in hot
sauce
excreted from the oil wells tinged with black tar and virulent
smoke.

On the sidewalk of shame, carrying the gentle bones of the
innocent,
trading them for a few pennies that sink deeper into angular
pockets.

From heaps of torn metal and welded bodies comes the
pungent aroma
of burning forests and lost seas. Pyres of carcasses in balding
fields.

Truths float down the river like slick oil layering the throat.
Adding measures of considerable ecstasy. Words now
commoditised.

The living— dying at the hands of the living, making a
cacophony of sounds that tickle the fancy of brutal capitalists.
Obfuscating reality.

Radiation induced erasure of thoughts; cutaneous
pigmentations blemish the fabric of ideas. Would you like a
snow globe of the climate crisis?

K B Ryan Joshua Mahindapala

What would Marie Kondo do[29]

I am ironing a dress I wore when I was 17,
When I tried it on two summers ago it fit perfectly.

It is tight on my chest, but it cinches at the waist,
with two bows and string that wrapped around

the back, then drops down just above my knees,
so when I spin around the room I feel like a film star.

It is black with spaghetti straps. I tend to prefer
capped-sleeves these days, tattoos peeking out,

but I love the white stars that polka-dot the dress.
I have always felt an affinity with the night sky,

and space. The last time I tried on the dress,
I wore it as a skirt, with a jumper on top to hide

the fact I couldn't do up the zip. I wonder
how much of my body is muscle and how much

is fat and how much is bone and what else I am made of.
I know I am heavier now, but maybe this is the body of a woman,

not a teenager, and it's okay that bodies change,
that doesn't make me bad; it just makes me a human being.

Carmina Masoliver

Aura[30]
For my fellow epileptics

The sort of depression
or exhaustion
where you take a nap
between the time
you drop
your eyeglasses
and when
you pick them up
again
.

And light returns
Eyes find objects
The motion of blurs
Doctors
Or nurses
Or both
Leaning over you
Smiling kind soft wet eyes—
"You're back."

Wayne Paul Mattingly

Calendar Walls And Green Circles[31]

For deliverance it seems we need
to say only, *We don't want* (or goodbye)
but we can't We've become inert much less noble.

For laughter or social emergencies
we substitute each other for breath.

The suspiration of our spirit is a promise familiar:
Our bed begot Hope. And in our scrubbed white tub
there was a soft fleshy baby with an inflatable duck
that had slowly lost its shape Between Comedy and Tragedy
this (image) is vacantly climactic but when that child turned
from toy to blue it would not be
for love. Our clear eyes were intractable.
Our spirit scraped clean.

What could we have wanted?
Or want now, other than this vacuum?

The walls of my study are lined with calendars
and each day with red pencil   I strike out
another, from the last day of my seventy-fifth year
backwards, seventy-five being an average lifetime.

When I stumbled from the bedroom to the study, I declared,
"When we're delivered a day, I mark one in green pencil."
It's a craziness, this calendar business, I know, and *should* be
confined.
I think of the men you would have impressed yourself upon,
had you known you'd be alone here.

Then just like that a note is sung or written

and the door I thought was locked, clicks—
quick splinters of light are flecked through my study
like the turns of finches and there's a gasp so deeply surprising
I can almost *feel* the air rush to you
before the light is sealed out again,
my sudden heart beaten like one of Audubon's birds
snapped into print—still

I go crazy with green circles.

Wayne Paul Mattingly

Ocean Beach[32]

I didn't know I could ever come back here
But the earth is round and as far as I can see
Out the city will circle round back to me

That's an ocean filling my eyes that once drowned
Me with its depth, its frightening darkness, fog-
Horns signaling peril, ships passing in the night

That was then. Here I sit in soft sand cross-
Legged, the horizon no different after a lifetime
While the city behind me—well, I won't turn around.

I was in love with those lights and sounds then
Now gone. But no one cares for nostalgia.
I'll tug the urge of memory through the sun-

Drenched waves, dapple my toes in surf, *remember*
All I can breathe in and out as the surf rustles
Over my sleepy body here in San Francisco.

Wayne Paul Mattingly

You Trees[33]

You trees got it right,
embarrassing us
with your test of time,
in which we are but a blip.
We *Homo sapiens*,
like fillies at the starting gate,
exploded into apparent success,
but now begin to falter.

You trees, who communicate
through miles of mycelial networks,
keep your young close,
move with exquisite slow meter
seeking only sunshine, rain and snow,
waiting for humans to pass,
like so many fallen leaves.

Jack Mayer

Music[34]

There are poems in us words cannot express.
Stanzas that are wrapped around our hearts
So tightly our souls can barely breathe,
And gasping for air,
We inhale rhythm.
Melodies that ease the ache,
Sliding between the stanza and the soul,
We breathe again,
And do not feel so alone.

Lily Mayo

Death Comes in Many Ways

Death comes in many ways;
Hands tied, shot in the head
with family you bore
victims of the cruel
brutality of war.

Death comes in many ways;
doctor with a syringe
maybe the most humane
to save a loved one from
more years of constant pain.

Death comes in many ways;
guiltily by own hand
a teenage mind derailed
another victim of
a system that has failed

Death comes in many ways;
The easiest must be
quietly in our sleep
after solemn prayer
asking our soul to keep.

Terry Miller

The day I see every day[35]

It was so horrifying everything turned a grainy, powdery grey,
my mouth went desert dry, then I was slobbering over the
cigarette
in my mouth, it went out and I let it drop to the bare concrete
floor,

I couldn't understand what I was seeing, my mind wouldn't
allow it past its
fire-wall, I saw but I didn't, the sight had shocked me to a
stand-still, my body wouldn't move although I wanted to run,
I was oddly angry that I hadn't made it through my life without
seeing
something like this,

The sight froze into a solid block in the corner of my mind, and
pops up like a jack-in-the-box and I stop dead, blink
everything into a noir crime scene,
I lurch into a catatonic state,
'Are you alive in there, mister?'
'I think so, I can't be sure'

Nothing makes an impression beyond that day, that sight in a
windowless
room on a stunning spring morning, I'd seen it and felt I'd been
seen seeing it,
and now I was part of it -

I'm silhouetted in the luminous doorway and they're scattered
around the
solemn space, caught in response-to-impact shapes, a room full
of skilled
contortionists, and me the audience

Keith Nunes

Eavesdropping

That was the winter of the Fagin gloves,
       Wedge heel boots and duffel coats
And Friday nights in the Fox and Hound;

The city bulged amber through slumped glass,
       The pavements grew slick with rain, and
Cool gathered in the folds of damp umbrellas.

Looking back, we could have been a painting,
       A Rembrandt perhaps, or a Vermeer:
The elements were there. See, the five of us huddled

At a table, leaning—not over dice, or a hand of cards—
       But towards one another, mid-sentence,
Firelight lacquering chins and knuckles, wetly;

Oils take days to dry. And there he is, still twenty-one,
       Slouched at the intersection of thirds,
His dark face flushed, hands upturned in supplication,

Perhaps, or anger—or had he just drunk too much beer?
       The face of the girl opposite is masked sheer
By the fall of her hair and the pale ridge of her ear,

But her shoulders are stiff, hands holding each other:
       Her whole body speaks. She can't see the waitress
Stepping out of the canvas, twisting back to look at her,

Drinks tray tilting; the others are settling into their
       Background for the night, the broad brushstrokes
Of their thoughts hardening. Only one is turned to us—

But enough. Let us go now, while there is still time
       Lest we eavesdrop too long on our own past,
And stir up ghosts to trail the rest of our lives.

Denise O'Hagan

Pietà[36]
After Perugino's Pietà (c. 1493)

And in the granite tenderness
        with which she lays her hand
over his long pale body laid out
        stiffly across her knees, is written
every mother's deepest fear, that it should
        come to this. She's set apart;
the portico around her makes sure of that,
        framing her in air. And yet—

There's something monolithic
        about her seated, blue-robed form
and sturdy spaced-apart knees, though
        her left hand curling his thigh is
fine boned, her little finger curving out and in
        like yours or mine; sometimes,
in these great works of art, it is
        the detail that we relate to.

Aware of her, we yet can't bring
        ourselves to face her. Instead, our eye
detours to the russet-haired and sandalled
        woman at her left, her fingers
steepling the bleached blades of his shins:
        this weeping Mary Magdalene,
cheeks reddened and glistening tears pearling,
        dares expose her undiluted grief.

Here's what we notice: the hair of St John
        brushing the bleeding face of Christ,
Nicodemus' eyes raised heavenwards
        as an aged Joseph of Arimathea rests
the hands that helped to bury him.
        But we are putty in the artist's hands,
and party to his formal composition,
        and drag our eyes at last to hers.

If we hoped to read them, we may think again.
          She's composed, has been for centuries,
and we are left to wrestle with the knowledge
          that this was always meant to be,
that part of her would have it no other way;
          the other part is left for us to fathom how
a blow unthinkable in human terms
          can in an oil painting be transformed.

Denise O'Hagan

Note: This poem draws its inspiration from the *Pietà* painted
by Pietro Perugino, the Italian Renaissance painter whose
compositions are well known for their classicism and formal
symmetry. Like the Michelangelo sculpture of the same name,
Perugino's painting depicts the Virgin Mary mourning over the
body of her son. Executed around 1483–1493, it was originally
painted for church of San Giusto alle Mura, outside
Florence,and is now housed in the Uffizi.

The orphan's pantoum

I looked at her, and she was there until she wasn't.
The stone was cold and dull where she had stood
And the space she'd occupied had lost its charge.
The moment dropped out of time and rolled away.

The stone was dull and cold where she had stood,
I'd shivered as I walked down the long corridor.
The moment dipped out of time and rolled away,
Her feet had hardly seemed to touch the floor.

I'd shivered as I walked back up the corridor
And I wondered if I had dreamed her after all,
Her feet had barely seemed to touch the floor.
Through the windows, snow was starting to fall.

I wondered if I had dreamed her, and yet I knew
That her eyes were grey and her dress was brown.
Through the windows, the snow had intensified
And silence lay coiled at the orphanage doors.

Her eyes were grey and her dress was brown.
She'd untied her gift of my fur-trimmed scarf
As silence lay coiled at the orphanage doors.
You gave me something of yourself, she'd said.

She had liked her gift of my fur-trimmed scarf.
But at home, I felt out of place and out of time.
You left me something of yourself, she'd said,
And holding it tight, she'd let no one come close.

But at home, I felt out of time and out of place.
My family seemed blurred as if through water,
I held myself tight, let none of them come close,
And thought why, when I spoke, didn't they hear?

My family seemed blurry as if through water.
Then rising, I stared at the mirror behind them
And knew why, when I spoke, they didn't hear:
My eyes were grey and my dress was brown.

Denise O'Hagan

Matariki[37]

As southern seasons spin their cycle
star cluster Matariki rises
birthed out of winter storm and darkness
glowing in the dawn sky.

Time to pause ...
for remembrance, reflection, renewal.

Give thanks for the months gone by
farewell those taken.
Celebrate the now—
our lives and loved ones.
Embrace the coming year
with hope and rekindled focus
while waiting for the kōwhai to signal
that winter is releasing its grip.

Helen Oliver

Never enough …[38]

Hunger for food
for touch
… for love.
Emptiness, hollowed out with want,
a void
propelling our quest.
Nurture of any kind
we seek
avidly …
unsated.
What is need, what is greed?
What is /
when is
ever
enough?

Helen Oliver

reflections at the end of the day[39]

flickering flames magnetise my gaze
glowing embers dazzle and spark
given a draught, the blaze fires up
voracious fire-fingers grasp and devour
mercilessly

in such a way, some people consume
those around them
vaporising all air/energy
blazing bright, overshadowing them
reducing them to cinders
amorphous, nondescript
—no phoenix to arise from such ashes

Helen Oliver

Soul[40]

Soul, spirit, self—all abide in me.

Self, seen here before you
in physical form, with all my frailties.

Spirit, my knowledge of the god-force,
my spiritual awareness.
Nothing to explain or justify—
each to their own.

Soul, ineffable, the essence of who I am—
invisible, intangible, beyond words.
Maybe this, the space within my heart,
is what may linger once I'm gone.

Helen Oliver

After the Argument[41]

Walking together yet   distanced.
Two hearts that are beating   unsynced.

Wooden bridges built over years
sway as we both walk   unbalanced.

Treading the same path over time
surely provides loves   evidence?

kintsugi-like each broken piece
must be glued with great   patience

united in a different form
and no longer live in   silence.

Rena Ong

Spilt Milk[42]

Birdsong outside penetrates through walls
trill notes celebrate the rising of dawn.

Two lovers inside stand apart unenthralled
Hearts shattered, eyes staring, shocked and forlorn,

recalling how he once whispered love words.
The bricks of defence that fell from her walls.

These hearts that once were united in all,
now broken, like glass-shards on cemented walls

His fingers extend, she in silence withdraws.
Too much blood spilt on glass cemented walls.

Rena Ong

Wordle[43]

Agile March races along river
Aging voice fades inmid paper

Crazy waves shoot above scale
Quiet names panic under smell

Leafy truth never stays still
Lawny April gaily plays about

Trees sadly await family alike
Reeds slyly place sense aside

Babies climb their glory cloud
Barns crown thine grave crowd

Jun Pan

How The Fish Feel[44]

How do fish feel
When the net is cast
Into their pond, or lake, or sea?
When their silvery shining
Is captured and entangled?
How do fish know
The meaning of danger?
In Zhenjiang, we walked along the banks
Of Yangtze River, where miles of water
Are laced with fishing nets.
We watched the fishermen
Pull in a net from the fish-pond.
Hundreds of fish were jumping.
They knew
The meaning of danger, even if
They did not know the exact recipe for dinner.
Zhao Jun told me that in Xinjiang
Or Tibet, in Western provinces,
The fish are not afraid.
It is easy to catch them.
What do the fish feel
When they feel fear?
Does their heart, like ours, beat faster?
What do the fish feel
In the restaurant aquarium
Watching the people dining, laughing,
As they wait to be eaten?
Do they dream of a delicious meal
Of people?
Looking at the fish on my plate, I imagine
That I am she, and the fish
Is the person.
The fish is smiling at me with teeth
That will bite me.
The fish looks at my head—
The most delicious part.
I have been steamed in a pot
With ginger and garlic.
The smell of my cooked flesh is wonderful.

I am a good meal.
In three minutes, I will cease to exist.

Joanna Radwańska-Williams
2 June 1997

Singing In The Messiah[45]

From where do these voices come?
The archangel countertenor
Was once a baritone, until
He discovered, one evening in Halle,
An outside voice within himself.
And how did the first angel sound
Upon that hill in Zion?
The music hall has become
A chamber in the space of Handel's voice.
The voices of our desire
Silently mouth the words.
There are echoes inside us
When we strain to comprehend
Whatever is perfect is God's.

Joanna Radwańska-Williams
15 December 1990

The Colour Of Water[46]

What I like most is the colour of water.
The deep azure.
The blue lagoon.
The white, pale blue and aquamarine
of Antarctic sea ice.
The undisturbed vastness of the Southern Ocean
where albatrosses roam.
The vibrant delights of the Great Barrier Reef.

Waterfalls and mountain streams,
their white rapids
roaring and bubbling away.
The slow meandering of mazy rivers
and apparent stagnation of the wetlands,
the realm of crabs and mudskippers.

Water runs through my fingers
from the kitchen tap.
I cannot live without it for a day.
My shower is my own private waterfall.
If I fill my bathtub to the rim with cold water,
its hue is pale aquamarine.

Joanna Radwańska-Williams
18 December 2021

we few[47]

flying far, perhaps,   birds might now sing   of
happiness   & elude the traps
bruising the sky.   is equality of existence
myth? sorry—I'm going

off again.   to the lake, sure as shit, the blood-red sun
always lies.   down
here   inside our starving hearts, truth's   tired revolving
doors   shut

over & over, unheeding   of gravity.   despots deny all
the planets'
spinning.   wary of exposure, their imperative orbits
keep score;

dividing the lower castes: we few.   we know (dreamers/
mothers/ poets):   fall
was when demi-gods fabricated fake gold.   supremacy's
entitlement   & sleights

mirror days past,   dangling like gore   in the talons of
a lazy osprey.
fate's raw smears   are marks of mockery…   sacrificial
chicks, they are: hubris,

creating outward   ripples.   crawling behind these
windowless   skies,
any blind soul   may shrink   & stifle whispers of hope.
fears

refute the lake's lucidity   with faulty logic.   dodging
reflection,
mountains with stars for crowns   press down   their
heavy bulk.   will cloud-

mountains with stars   for crowns press   down?
their heavy bulk will cloud/
refute the lake's lucidity   with faulty logic.   dodging
reflection,

any blind soul may   shrink & stifle whispers   of
hope/ fears,
creating   outward ripples.   crawling behind
these windowless skies,

fate's raw smears are marks   of mockery; sacrificial
chicks.   they are hubris'
mirror.   days past, dangling   (like gore in the talons
of a lazy osprey),

was when demi-gods fabricated fake gold/ supremacy's
entitlement   & sleights
dividing   the lower castes.   we few, we know
dreamers.   mothers (poets) fall;

spinning;   wary   of exposure/ their imperative.
orbits keep score
over & over.   unheeding of gravity, despots   deny all.
the planets?

here, inside   our starving hearts.   truth's tired.
revolving doors shut
off again to the lake.   sure as shit, the blood-red sun
always lies down,

bruising the sky.   is equality of existence   myth?
sorry,   I'm going…
flying far.   (perhaps birds might?)   now: sing of
happiness, & elude   the traps!

kerry rawlinson

night holds us inside earth's black body divine, her magic black hat of implicate reality wherein, inside black window-lanterns hung from now invisible dark tree branches, we plant lighted raindrop candles, seeds of peace for the Lunar New Year—

Xuan Wu Lake's black waves float more raindrops of candlelight to seed reconciliation—

Guan Yin, born hot white lotus anchored, afloat under Ice Moon, is quickly moving viridian water tucking pink lilies behind her ear; each palm's eye reflects fourteen lifelines; between fingers, silences of moon open fragrances of wood—

lifted into vertical, epichronic time, our head-tops are seeds floating to the temple of riddles strung on long ribbons from lanterns, each a puzzle inviting multiple answers—

I draw: *make of yourself a light*— impossible!—drawing me back into the cool dark and deep mediation well of St. John's chapel where memory's sun-blessing drama replays—

Act 1 begins through honeycomb windows as 6 AM sun fire kindles tangerine tulip fire, until twelve inner lights flare up from each still point—

Act 2 continues through honeycomb windows as sun fire quickens inner light curling up inside bud-faced monks until their worker-bee faces are glowing rice paper lanterns—

Act 3 is a heart gradually opening as E.E. Cummings chants *nobody beautiful hurries*—

Act 4 begins outdoors just as the sun's amber-flamed hand that caresses my face also caresses the face of fresh-water lakes, touches Lake Superior tossed water-polished agates until they sparkle the shore, warms powder and grit sand, pierces the compact bite of granite rising to sharp peaks, comforts the dove-grey stone of wavy lake-side seats, thrills scallops of Arborvitae, embraces pungent needles of white pine—

Act 5 follows the sun's creative movement purpling crocus, still cupping snow in coned crowns, while preparing brown-furred magnolia buds to break open their fragrant white and pink treasures—

Act 6 calls me to remember the tiny immensely intense blue light rising from within me, restarting my breath, waking me from near death— that tiny particle of light so much greater than i am— a seed-light initiating peace and reconciliation to which i bow—

Act 7 finds me reverencing what is impossible, yet what lights up within me. i am medium of eccentric messages— seeds growing into fuller inspirations yet to be harvested at Mid-Autumn Moon—

M. Ann Reed

I Didn't Know the Last Time was the Last Time

Would that we were together still
In our own Forever, still

How many times can a heart break
How much can one endure heartache...

I hear the sound of your key in the door
But you're not there
The whisper of your voice in my ear
But you're not there
Your fingertips tapping a beat on the table
But you're not there
Your distinctive snore in the middle of the night
But you're not there

How was I to know
That the last time we touched, we spoke, we hugged, we
laughed,
would be the last time
    ...Ever

Tell me where to look, tell me how to hear;
Tell me what to see, so I know you're still here

My eyes cry for you, my voice calls for you
My hands reach for you, my heart longs for you

Let me hold you
    Will you hold me
Let me touch you
    Will you touch me
Let me hear your voice
    Will you hear mine too

Let me find you
    You can find me…

I'm here, I'm here, I'm here
I wish that you were, too

Vinni Relwani

Epiphany[49]

Everywhere I go
spring comes
plowing through the earth
the green thrust of grass
of narcissus and daffodils
into sunlight
as well as chill breezes.

Spring comes
like prayers
rising through the stem
like cream that rises on milk
like snow angels
planted in winter.

Morning streams
on bare branches
transforms
the nothing there
with a glaze of light
a promise . . .

Allegra Jostad Silberstein

Recovery and Renewal[50]

Though the attacker had ripped pride from her psyche,
    she vowed to restore it.
Though frowns replaced radiance on her face,
    she declared she'd regain it.
Though her shoulders drooped from fallen
    self-esteem, she would lift them again.
Shame and fear smeared her mirror, but commitment could
wipe it clean.
    She must not live a slave to depression and bitterness.
She would come alive again, like a bright, bold crocus in
spring.
    And so she told her body, her mind and soul every day,
    I will rise again like a Phoenix.
She affirmed her growth every morning,
    I am becoming healthy, lovely, worthy, resilient and
strong.

Visioning proved a syntax of healing. Reciting words when she
couldn't
    yet believe them, claiming hope when she couldn't feel
it,
    praising sunshine when she couldn't see it.
When energy sagged, or perseverance flagged, when
roadblocks
piled high like rocky mountains, she leaned on shoulders
    of friends, and sometimes cried.
But tears flushed doubts and miracles began to bloom
    like cheerful daffodils in March.
Faith flowered as she practiced it. Certainty took root
    as she plodded the treadmill of therapy.
Courage grew as she ventured out. Confidence rose
    as she stopped recoiling at a tender touch.
Forever wounded, her scars remained, but dimmed and
receded.
    One day she stood at the spotless mirror and admired
her radiant smile. Her heart knew she would
    now be well and whole, and embrace the future.

Wesley Sims

The fountain still falls

Is there a place one can turn to, can run to and find?
A sentient place,
perhaps of the mind?

A place that will know, without whispers or telling,
the secrets of heart, the regrets, still a-welling,
unbidden, abiding, like founts of cognition?
Not bursting or brimming or forcing contrition,
but there, still there, that trickle, that drop, that gush of salt rush
that seldom will stop?

Will this place know, without being told, my joys and my
angst? Or each truth that I hold?
What about
residing of hope—or suspension of fears?
Of wholehearted love,
or spinning of years of strange thoughts to luminous threads?
The logical lust for a weave that embeds
thoughtful action into redoubling sight—
when no wrong's purely wrong,
nor right, simply right?

The fountain still falls, at the back of cognition,
and there, somewhere there, is the faint recognition, that there's
a side room, too,
to this sentient space,
where an equal, full heart, is looking to trace the *underside*
weave (or opposite etching),
till perception and truth, the ones we've been sketching,
unlink and unlace,
beguile, perhaps blend,
in this room of renewal, this place without end…
and if it is sentient, then it's all knowing:
if it has wisdom,
it'll surely be showing…
invite her to stay—
lead me there now.

Hayley Solomon

You'll be dipping at shadows

Joy is transient—recognize her immediately, laugh with her
lightly.
Allow touches of traces to linger when
she inevitably trips away,
to some
other space.

True joy is too poignant to grasp or to grip;
don't try, you'll be dipping at shadows when you clasp her,
for she slips away the very second
you fear her
ephemerality.

For where there is desperation, there can be no joy—
antithesis, so quick to sully,
alloys
with swift cruelty.
Now, it is easier to project loss, than to lean into perfection.

A rare moment, delight—inexpressibly bright.

Bask in the brilliance of it, safe in the certainty she'll transition
away kindly,
leaving sufficient trails of memory to soothe
her passing.

Know that Joy's trailing kindness can be as elastic or as brittle
as you make it, lingering long,
or breaking brutally,
sensitive—
always sensitive—
to your intent.

With ineffable gentleness, treasure her gifted trails—you might
then find Harmony.

Hiding shyly in Harmony, is Hope, simple Hope,
and peeking from *her* are the fair, twinkling eyes of Happiness.

Happiness is sweeter than Joy, and so much less fleeting, *if*
you invite her to stay.

Hayley Solomon

Alone in Germany[51]

She sits on the couch, absently stroking the cat on her lap,
trying to lose herself in some mindless TV show.
Giving up, she switches off the set, picks up a book,
but that doesn't hold her attention for long.

She turns on the radio, finds a classical music station,
finally relaxes when she hears a cello.

He plays the cello, travels throughout the country.
Where is he now? She has his itinerary,
but comfortably ensconced on the couch with the cat,
she doesn't want to get up and look for it.

She doesn't care.
No matter where he is, she aches to have him by her side,
longs for him to play his music only for her.

After a while, tired of wallowing in self pity,
disentangling herself from couch and cat, she finds paper and
pencil,
sits down at her desk, starts writing a poem.

Abbie Taylor

In the Bowling Alley[52]

A college kid with a visual impairment,
I stand at the edge of the lane,
feet planted behind black line,
knees bent, ball in right hand,
swing right arm back and forth to gain momentum,
let fly as arm moves forward.

With a thunk, the ball hits the lane,
rolls slowly and methodically out of my line of vision.
After an eternity, for the first time,
my classmates' cheers fill the air,
as all upright pins connect with ball,
hit the floor with a satisfying clatter.

Abbie Taylor

Now That You're Gone[53]

I'm a writer who carries out a lone existence,
as I did ten years ago before we married.
I no longer struggle to find writing time.
I wake up, check email,
eat breakfast, write, work out,
write some more, eat lunch,
check email again, write some more,
end the day with Dr. Pepper, more e-mail
and social media,,eat dinner,
recline with a good book, magazine, or podcast,
go to bed, think of you, wish you were here.
Life goes on.

Abbie Taylor

Watching the Dusk on a Rainy Night: Musing[54]

Watching the dusk:
clouds painted over the
foggy mountains
in a sfumato style,
as teacher suggested,
with coloured pencils scraps
pressed over within the lines
by tiny fingers.
Do not cry over the past!
Take that little pupil you were
in your arms and toss him in the air
Every child loves that!
Then make a paper ball of those memories
and throw it around.
Memories as notes
and you the composer

The mountains darken,
dusk already brings night.
Let the rains cry for you
and fertilize the soil
where flowers will grow
with their corollas facing the sun
delivering you a song of joy
A song that will not leave you
Wherever you may go
Its notes like bells
Filling the air in silence

Luisa Ternau

Upsala Glacier[55]

The Upsala glacier
is dying
as I hike along the shore
of Lake Argentino
and hear the painful groans of its
bones cracking
in the Andean wind.

As I approach
the surviving ice
shattered rock
and graveyard quiet
warns me
I stare at the
detritus of its
demise.

In the distance
near Upsala's icy shards
the spikey rocks appear black
in the cloud filtered
sun light
as I follow
their procession towards me
the blackness blends into
multiple hues of grey
which endures for
a few yards
then changes
to many shades of browns
and rusts and tans
the autumn leaves
of my childhood.

Strewn
among the rock
a few miniature
green plants
in a primal struggle

for life
have gained hold
attempting to live and spread
in the carcass of the glacier.

The wind and rain and
heat with a jackal-like
ferocity
constantly assault
the glacier.

Gasping
it surrenders and leaves
stones for the earth and
tears for me.

Edward Tiesse

A Shakespearean Insight

Shakespeare said
Men are the measure of all things,
But some men believe that they are
The measure of all men and superior kings.
In every tribe, nation, and republic,
Are those ambitious guys
Who do not have a satisfied ambition
Unless they can always rise and rise
Above the crowds that want food, wine, love and a peaceful
nation.
In some countries there is a lonely killer
Who is happy to kill thousands and destroy every city
To show that he has the power
To rule for infinity.
Some other leaders say
They want to make their country great,
But do not understand that all they do
Is make their country grate.
So human society faces this threat
Of nations led by men with ambitions
That endangers the peace of all who live
In a world dominated by lies and seditions.
So if we lived on a little island
Where no one thought they had a global role
We could enjoy a life of peace and pleasure,
And never fear that there was a politician in control
Who wanted to use extensive conflicts that lead to war
To show the world he was a life-long king
Who gave his people a sense that they were in a land of
pleasures galore.
But we don't live on a little island,
We all live on places that are part of a global world.
We need to talk with neighbours near and far
So that we can live undisturbed
By the fears and fantasies spread
By political personae who want to be on top
Until all their rivals are dead.

Roger Uren

Morning Mist[56]

Brushes against a soft white cloud of feather-down.
A gentle breeze sweeps the room as a blanket floats up and
down.
I close my eyes and breathe.

A feather flutters and lands in my hand.
It tickles as I swoosh it away.
A sweet mist of vanilla and cinnamon soothe the senses.

A crisp cool air breezes through an open window as bird-song
fills the atmosphere.
A warm-golden ray of delight enters through gaps in the
curtains.
It energizes my soul.

A warm aroma of caramel latte travels the house and greets me
eagerly.
A sigh of relief, I am happy.
I am home.

Anna Verhaegh

A City Full of You

Meeting you gave me the permission
I sought in myself.
To get out & explore in a sense
that it feels like home.
Being with you, the best idea yet.
Small petite buildings, towering
buildings.
Everyday feels brand new
I don't feel the need to stay cooped
up inside a room.
With you I want to get out &
explore and sleep when there is
time.
I've never been to a place like
this before.
I've never tasted food this good
before & for once,
There are no distractions, no other
place to be.
The lights that shine from your eyes
The thoughts that travel fast like cars.
I've never been to a city like this
before, the best idea yet.
When people ask me where I've been
I call your name.
When friends ask me where I'm going
I call your name.
And I can't wait until I get back there

Kewayne Wadley

Flat Blue Sheets

I come to life when you touch me
Fluent & continuous.
You've unzipped my lips and tossed
them to the side.
I've never fallen &
been caught so freely.
I've never paid attention to how
flat the world really was.
A jagged peninsula
Eloped in oceans embrace
Curved in explosion.
Sometimes it feels like I am
Drowning.
I've never paid attention to how
flat the world really is
Chipped off & covered
falling deeper into you

Kewayne Wadley

Home Sweet Home

Home sweet home
Home sweet home
It sure feels good to be
home again.

Been away for so long,
Almost forget what coming
home feels like.
Down the street, I am almost there.
The place I know best.
The place I put above all else,
There's no place I'd rather be.
Sweet girl like you.
The warm embrace of being missed.

After so many miles the end
is drawing near.
Home sweet home
Home sweet home.
Soon as I am there, I'll kiss the welcome
mat of your feet &
recline deep in the chair of your arms.
Soon as I am there I'll sink into comfort,
I'll pour me a glass filled in your kiss.
The warm embrace of being missed.
It sure feels good to be home again.
Dozing off fast asleep at home.
Safe & sound in your arms

Kewayne Wadley

Petite Roses

If I could slide myself into the
Palm of your hands.
I'd split myself into five slender
stems,
So all of me could fit into the
Vase of your hands.
Between the stems there is
A piece of me that I've hidden,
Wild in proximity to you.
Between your thumbs
I've succumbed to the tenderness
of your smile.
Though petite, my day is no
longer incomplete.
So I took a seat, and watched
the sun rise from your smile
for just a while longer

Kewayne Wadley

When You Paint

When you touch me
Everything turns right side up.
My down is no longer
The same.
I suffocate in colour
My body between your hands.
You squeeze me tight,
My hobby becoming yours.
You've shaken me dry &
Soaked my dreams.
My world made that much brighter.
No matter how much paint
I have to wash out of my hair.
When you paint
Everything turns right side up
No matter what colour you use

Kewayne Wadley

Ma-ly[57]

Amber, Amber, Thunderstorm
Cactus flowers bloom.

A primary school never heard before
Which I totally ignore.

Self-introduction, reading passages
Interview, interview, interview
Awaiting in the auditorium are lots of faces.

Thunderstorm, Amber, Red
Aneurysm, BBA, LCA, Stent
Headaches forced me to go to bed.

The Planets
What a Happy Day!
Boogie-Woogie Goose

The unpredictable weather
Cactus flowers wither.

Thunderstorm, Amber, Red
Waterspout in Cheung Chau reported

Where are the hairy crab babies?

Honghua Wang

Unfolding 2022[58]

I saw a sparrow today on the sidewalk
before the big crossroad near a hospital
The sparrow danced on the weeds,
looking so comfortable
and leaving me a little shock.

Blue sky, gurgling stream,
Green mountain, fragrant jasmine,
All buried in a dream.

Motorcycles with deliverymen wearing a mask
Familiar on-line classes through Zoom
A family barbecue behind a truck
A city filled with gallantry and gloom

The noisy emptiness

Time is there.
Time is not there.

Honghua Wang

Boy on a Boat

A blue-white windy day of hard-edged clarity.
An open-decked spree for a schoolboy gang at sea,
who fall about like loose cannon balls rolling every which-way
with the heave and pitch of the boat on a lively sea.
I'm there to stop them hurtling over the side

to an early and watery death. But this day of untidy
arms and legs and flying ties, this day is one for good will—
so that won't happen. From the downstairs deck
on unsteady hands and knees clambers up a happy boy.
In years past he'd be "simple" to well-meaning souls,

or simply locked away. Not this boy in his vivid red coat,
bold in a sea of cool blazer blue and wild wind.
Following the lurching of the boat he staggers and pitches
from boy to boy, hugging each in turn for balance or joy, or
both,
grinning with his face on a neck or a woolen breast.

He sees this as his absolute right, one strong enough for
normally
untouchable boys to forget to be monsters
and push Other away. His dauntless will
and singular ardour for this wind-blown coddled crew
binds him to us with a sailor's knot, one never learned and
rarely taught.

When we dock will our return to hard-land sense
give us back to Difference? Or in our journeys
after this—in storm or calm—will memory hold
the effervescence of that one bright heart,
a keeper of secrets well beyond our ken?

George Watt

Christmas 1953

His long, grey beard feathers my hand
as he bends to his sack.
In awe, I clutch the bright present
and sidle back to watch
others approach this herald
of mystery, promise and plenty.

Two days later with parents out,
my bold, older brother
takes me to barred, brown closet doors.
They creak open to smells
of stale tobacco and hair oil.
A rich red velvet gown

hangs over full-sized wellies
cotton wool glued tops.
A disembodied beard hangs limp.
A brown box of Durex
Sits atop a bright orange book:
Lady Chatterley's Lover.

"What is Durex and who is she?"
My brother's evasive reply:
"She's a lady, who talks a lot."
But this *non-sequitur*
can't trump the exposure of my dad
as a phony Father Christmas.

Yet the most vexing thing that wasn't right?
The beard! It wasn't fluffy, and far from white.

George Watt

Lot & His Daughters[59]
    —Genesis 19: 30-38

Escaped! Forbidden to turn or look back
at the terrible conflagration.
No one could survive this blitz
on unrighteousness, on evil, on sin.

With their mother still salty and cooling,
in our coal-black cave my daughters huddle,
coaxing new flame from dull smoking embers,
a falling shawl exposing one plump breast.

They glance back over half-bare shoulders
hoping I was too drunk to recall
their conquest. And what did they do after?
Hid my nakedness with my old prayer shawl.

Now granite bedded, decorously draped,
I'm the subject after an old master,
who, in his work, paints sufficient attire
too allow for, yet to quench desire.

What to think? I'm saved from one cataclysm
to suffer this heat of a carnal kind
from my own daughters, svelte and lissom,
at the command of an exacting God.

Or is this revenge, for I offered them—
my daughters—to slate the licentious lust
of the scrofulous mob who'd have their way
with the angels. I did what must be done.

Accept my sin as venal when compared
To gruesome perverts humping the divine.
Over the hills and the wide desert sands
blows the acerbic scent of their roasting.

Nestling over there by the fire, are they
plotting another round? I'll think on that,
the only virtuous man alive. Rest!
We—God and I—still have a bond in trust:

Lot's God: God's Lot. We are as good men are,
select members of the cosmic boys' club.
He did watch over our fervent coupling.
I wonder? Was he bemused (or aroused)?

Then he took off, unseen on desert winds,
cooling sulphurs, embers, sending saline
puffs from the warm surface of a pillar
that used to be something, or someone else.

George Watt

Possession & Dispossession
> *After Hilda Doolittle, 'Sea Rose'*
> *and William Blake, 'The Sick Rose'.*

That tiny, weightless pile of pink-black
used to be a rose
infected
consumed.
You wormed your way in,
and after with a blunt blade
gouged another notch
on your serpentine belt.

As you keep score.
Facing you, this new rose,
this sea rose
chose the feverish tide.
What you crave, away!—
so here—on land (or in sense)—
her warm fragrance
her soft pink textures

are but might-have-been.
So foam at the mouth as you try to wring
dead life from that thick leather belt,
grunt as the blunt blade
trembles in your impotent hand,
curse with the memory of her cracking stem
and her out-of-reach fragility.
For her there was no looking back

to your on-shore fire
burning with drift-wood in dunes
between land and sea,
between madness and sanity.
Now she is lost to you,
and found only in foam and sea,
and she's free—thank God!—
from you… or me.

George Watt

The Waiting Room

The only really interesting thing is what
happens between two people in a room.
       —Francis Bacon

Then. A shabby room. Your face, fragile, pale
in the meagre light from frosted windows,
leaden and dusty. Your gaze in the gloom—
cool, direct, inquisitive. Mine evades,
darts from ceiling to floor to black fly-spots
on dog-eared magazines. You talk a lot.
I try, but excitement smothers effort.
You are first called, but as you leave the room
you tuck your address into my pocket.
No name. We never said. No phone number.

After feverish days of fantasy,
Courage finds me in an almost empty bus
taking me to your grand gothic mansion,
where sun's rays flash on aristocratic windows
through breeze-brushed boughs of grand trees.
The oak doors are black, forbidding. When open
who will condemn this intense boy knocking
on a man's business? Parents? Maid? You?
Fearing an answer, I turn round and walk
unwillingly towards what-might-have-been.

Now. Old and grey, and nodding by the fire,
with a chronic ache for a lost love? No.
None of that. The room that held me for an hour
I hold within—always have and always will—
and in its heart, sitting warm, is a knot
of sensuousness, of hope, and untouchable joy.

George Watt

Honest Toil[60]

slashing that paddock of dry summer grasses
          letting the sun in to germinate new feed
          for the winter to follow the encroaching
autumn

          you bounce on the metal seat of the
Massey Ferguson
          describing the four sides of the paddock's
perimeter
          long lines swathed you turn and turn again
          taking pride in the straightness of your line

          you close on the central square
          which marks completion of this job
          dozens of field mice corralled in that
diminishing island
          make a desperate break across the mown
paddock

          the goshawk hovers

          next year you know
          start in the centre and work outwards
          to deny the predator

Michael Witts

Of the Floating World[61]

Great wave off Kanagawa
First of thirty-six views of Mount Fuji
          — Hokusai Museum Nagano

I

memory erodes
an artisan's knife taken to the woodblock
whittling away at the artist's sketch
leaving nothing of the template

II

each layer pressed with ink
or washed with paint
the emerging accumulation
of that dark blue sea

III

wind spumed wave leaning to
imminent crash
maritime fingers animating a cartoon malice

IV

then three boats ten manned
emerge through surf
terror or exhilaration bends them to their work
of keeping these boats heading out to sea

V

in the foreground
a conical white wave erupts
against the darkening sea

VI

in the background like an echo
Mount Fuji sunstruck against the sky
on that stormy morning

VII

each print an evolution
as the woodblock degrades
with each printing

Michael Witts

Transmogrification[62]

cooler nights of late summer
bring a stillness to the pond
the abyss reflects your face
and a swirling universe of stars

the stubborn low dumps rain
that won't let up   the pool quickens
with call and response
a blackness to swallow you

the cauldron curdles with writhing bodies
the desperate uncaring act of reproduction
competing to replicate with random mates
before the opportunity expires

frogspawn erupting in clotted clumps
each egg a proto tadpole
water clogged with life as
the frogs depart and silence returns

wriggling spermatozoa compete for space
commence the slow transition
dropping tails and acquiring legs
to leap from that heaving ooze

then to wait out the next dry spell
in some damp mothering crack
before emerging basso profundo
to crank up that urgent song

Michael Witts

THE POETS

The following brief biographies are based on texts provided by the poets. As there is an interval of months between the submission of brief biographies and the editing of the Anthology, much may have changed in the meantime.

VINITA AGRAWAL is the author of four books of poetry: *Two Full Moons* (Bombaykala Books), *Words Not Spoken* (Brown Critique), *The Longest Pleasure* (Finishing Line Press) and *The Silk Of Hunger* (AuthorsPress). Vinita is an award-winning poet, editor, translator and curator, based in Indore, India. Joint Recipient of the Rabindranath Tagore Literary Prize 2018, and winner of the Gayatri GaMarsh Memorial Award for Literary Excellence, USA, 2015. She is Poetry Editor with *Usawa Literary Review*. She edited an anthology on climate change titled *Open Your Eyes* (Hawakal) in 2020. She also edited a Memoir-Anthology on the Kashmiri poet Ghulam Rasool Nazki in 2021 (Ink Links). Most recently she co-edited the *Yearbook of Indian Poetry in English 2020-21* (Hawakal). She is on the Advisory Board of the Tagore Literary Prize.   She is also on the Global Judging Panel of the SheInsprawrds.

JOY C. AL-SOFI is a published writer of poetry, fiction and non-fiction. Originally from the USA, where she was a practicing attorney, she has been teaching English in Hong Kong since 2004.

SHIKHA BANSAL has worked in the publishing industry for several years both in India and Hong Kong. She currently resides in India.

ALAN BERN is a retired Children's Librarian from the Berkeley Public Library. He worked in public libraries in the San Francisco Bay Area for over 25 years in a variety of jobs. He is a poet, storywriter, and photographer and has two books of poetry published by Fithian Press: *No no the saddest* (2004) and *Waterwalking in Berkeley* (2007). A third book of poetry, *greater distance and other poems* (2015), was published by his own press, Lines & Faces, a press and publisher specializing in illustrated poetry broadsides, collaborating with the artist Robert Woods, linesandfaces.com. Alan was a runner up for The Raw Art Review's The John H. Kim Memorial Short Fiction Prize for his story 'The alleyway near the downtown library'; and he won a medal from SouthWest Writers for his story 'The Return of the Very Fierce Wolf of Gubbio to Assisi, 1943 CE [and now, 2013 CE]' and his poem 'Boxae' was first runner-up for the Raw Art Review's first Mirabai Prize for Poetry, 2020. He was also a finalist in the NCWN's 2019 Thomas Wolfe Fiction Prize; he won the Littoral Press Poetry Prize in 2015; and he was a semi-finalist in the 2016 Center for the Book Arts Poetry Chapbook Competition. Alan has poems, stories, and photos published in a wide variety of online and print publications, from which his work has been nominated for Pushcart Prizes. Recent photos published include: unearthedesf.com/alan-bern, feralpoetry.net/four-haiga-by-alan-bern/, and pleaseseeme.com/issue-7/art/alan-bern-art-psm7/. Alan is also a performer working with the dancer Lucinda Weaver as PACES: dance & poetry fit to the space and with musicians from Composing Together.

MARIA ELENA BLANCO (Havana, Cuba) Poet, essayist and translator who writes predominantly in her native Spanish. Having spent a good part of her formative years in New York, has also developed her own English poetic voice, mainly through the practice of translation. She has taught French literature and language and worked for the United Nations as translator/reviser, presently on a freelance basis. She frequently participates in international poetry festivals and literary colloquia and her poetry has been translated into all major Romance languages, also into English, German, Greek and Chinese, among others. Her published work includes poetry collections *Posesión por pérdida* (Seville: Barro and Santiago, Chile: Libra, 1990), *Corazón sobre la tierra / tierra en los Ojos* (1998), *Alquímica memoria* (2001), (Madrid: Betania, 2001), *Mitologuías* (Madrid: Betania, 2001), *danubiomediterráneo /mittelmeerdonau* (Vienna: Labyrinth, 2005, Spanish-German), *El amor incontable* (Madrid: Vitrubio, 2008), Havanity / Habanidad (Miami: Baquiana, 2010, English-Spanish), *Escrito en lenguas* (Chile: Verbodesnudo, 2015) *Sobresalto al vacío* (Chile: Mago, 2015), *Botín* (Leiden: Bokeh, 2016) and *Oro vano* (Chile: Verbodesnudo, 2018), as well as a collection of textual analyses of selected poetry and prose works, *Asedios al texto literario* (Madrid: Betania, 1999), and a volume of critical essays on Cuban themes, *Devoraciones. Ensayos de período especial* (2016). She has recently published an acclaimed Spanish verse translation of Charles Baudelaires *Les fleurs du mal* (Santiago, Chile/Madrid: RIL, 2021) and has translated Austrian poets Marie-Thérèse Kerschbaumer, Gerhard Kofler and Heidi Pataki into Spanish. Winner of First (2019), Second (2016) and Third (2017, 2018) prizes in the International Proverse Poetry Prize (Single Poems), Hong Kong, as well as other international poetry distinctions. She divides her time between her homes in Vienna, Santiago, New York and the Andalusian countryside.

GAVIN BOURKE grew up in the suburb of Tallaght in West Dublin. Married to Annemarie living in County Meath, he holds a B.A. in Humanities from Dublin City University, an M.A. Degree in Modern Drama Studies and a Higher Diploma in Information Studies from University College Dublin. His work broadly covers nature, time, memory, addiction, mental health, human relationships, the inner and outer life, creating meaning and purpose, politics, contemporary and historical social issues, injustice, the human situation, power and its abuse, absurdism, existentialisms, human psychology, cognition, emotion and behaviour, truth and deception, the sociological imagination, illness, socio-economics, disability, inclusivity, human life, selfishness and its consequences as well as urban and rural life, personal autonomy, ethics, commerce, science, grand schemes and the technological life in English and to a lesser extent in the Irish Language.

LAWRENCE BRIDGES is best known for work in the film and literary world. His poetry has appeared in *The New Yorker*, *Poetry*, *The Tampa Review*, and *Ambit*. He has published three volumes of poetry: *Horses on Drums* (Red Hen Press, 2006), *Flip Days* (Red Hen Press, 2009) and *Brownwood* (Tupelo Press, 2016). He created a series of literary documentaries for the National Endowment for the Arts 'Big Read' initiative, which includes profiles of Ray Bradbury, Amy Tan, Tobias Wolff and Cynthia Ozick. He lives in Los Angeles.

LINA BUIVIDAVICIUTE was born on May 14, 1986. She has a BA in Lithuanian philology and advertising, and a MA in Lithuanian literature. She is a poet, literary scholar and literary critic. Her first poetry book *Helsinki Syndrome* was published in 2017.

SEAN CAMSHON is a primary school teacher from New Zealand who has never published, let alone submitted any writing for publication.

CAROL FLAKE CHAPMAN was formerly a journalist. She returned to poetry, her first love, after the sudden death of her husband on a wild river in Guatemala shattered her life. Poetry, she found, was the language of healing and of connection to the natural world. She has written two books of poetry, and she has performed her poems in gatherings around the world.

TOM CHOI was born in 1995. He made an acquaintance with Shakespeare's Sonnets when he was an undergrad. Later he signed up for a programme in Literary and Comparative Studies at HKBU. *To Modern Fables* (Hong Kong: Sino United Electronic Publishing Ltd., 2022) is his debut collection of poetry.

WILLIAM LEO COAKLEY has published in magazines and anthologies in America, China, England, and Ireland, including *London Magazine* and the *Paris Review*, and he often gives public readings. His poems have won awards from the Sotheby's International Poetry Competition, Yeats Society, and New England Poetry Club (for a Cavafy translation). He is publisher of Helikon Press. A Bostonian and an Irish citizen, he was on the shortlist for the New Irish Writing Prize in 2019 and 2020.

SUZANNE COTTRELL is the author of three poetry chapbooks: *Gifts of the Seasons, Autumn and Winter*; *Gifts of the Seasons, Spring and Summer*; and *Scarred Resilience* (Kelsay Books). Her poems have appeared in numerous journals and anthologies. She lives with her husband in central, rural North Carolina. She is an outdoor enthusiast and retired teacher, who enjoys reading, hiking, knitting, Pilates, and yoga.

JULIO CESAR DIAZ, a Texas-born Centroamericano, lives in Massachusetts. Diaz is a gay bilingual left-handed Capricorn, who uses he/them pronouns. He has received scholarships from Bread Loaf Translators' Conference, Palm Beach Festival, and Juniper Institute. His work has appeared in *North American Review, Southword Journal*, and *Barrio Writers*.

NEIL DOUGLAS is a doctor who has worked as a GP and a Community Paediatrician in London's East End. He is an enthusiastic member of the Covent Garden Stanza poetry collective affiliated with the Poetry Society and has published work in the UK, North America and Hong Kong. In 2020 he was longlisted for the Poetry Society's National Poetry Competition and in 2021 was shortlisted for the Bridport Prize. He is currently studying for an MA in Creative and Life Writing at Goldsmiths, University of London.

AHMED ELBESHLAWY is a scholar of comparative literature, author, and poet. His books include *Unappeasable Ghosts* (Yorkshire Publishing, 2021), *Savage Charm* (Proverse Hong Kong, 2019), *Twenty Five Meditations on Writing and Subjectivity* (London Academic Publishing, 2019), *Woman in Lars von Trier's Cinema* (Palgrave, 2016), *America in Literature and Film* (Routledge, 2011). His other publications include various articles and book chapters in *The Palgrave Handbook of Literature and the City* (2016), *Sexuality and Culture* (2014), *The Comparatist* (2008), *Scope* (2008), and *fe/male bodies* (2005, 2006).

DEAN GESSIE is an author and poet who has won dozens of international awards and prizes. Among other honours, Dean was included in The 64 Best Poets of 2018 and 2019 by Black Mountain Press in North Carolina. He also won the Aesthetica Creative Writing Award in England, the Allingham Arts Festival Poetry Competition in Ireland and the Creators of Justice Literary Award [Fiction Category] from the International Human Rights Art Festival in New York. Elsewhere, Dean won the Frank O'Hara Poetry Prize in Massachusetts, the Enizagam Poetry Contest in California, the Ageless Authors Poetry Contest in Texas, the Indigo Open Poetry Prize in England, the Spoon River Review Editors'

Prize in Illinois, the Southern Shakespeare Company Sonnet Contest in Florida, the COP26 Poetry Competition in Scotland and the UN-aligned Poetry Contest in Finland [in honour of the U.N. Climate Change Conference]. Dean's short story collection—called Anthropocene—won an Eyelands Book Award in Greece and the Uncollected Press Prize in Maryland. He has a book of poetry forthcoming [goat song] from Uncollected Press.

OLGA GONZALEZ LATAPI (she/her/hers) is a queer poet with an MFA in Writing from California College of the Arts. Although her writing journey started in journalism, she is now pursuing her true passion: exploring the world of poetry with a mighty pen in hand. She got her BS in Journalism at Northwestern University. Her work has been published in *Teen Voices Magazine*, *Sonder Midwest literary arts magazine*, BARNHOUSE Literary Journal, *Wild Roof Journal*, *Impossible Task*, *Genre: Urban Arts*, *Biscuitroot Drive*, iaam.com, and *The Nasiona Magazine*. She is the translator of the upcoming *Reflections of an Old Man* (Pensamientos de un Viejo) by Colombian philosopher Fernando González, as well as a spoken word album with Amaryllis Recordings. Originally from Mexico City.

CASEY HAMPTON is a poet and fiction writer currently residing in the Pacific Northwest. His work has appeared in *Dialogue*, *Entropy*, *Star 82 Review*, *Euphony Journal* and elsewhere. When not writing, he helps out on the family farm and spends as much time as he can with his coonhound Josie.

SADIE KAYE is a Hong Kong TV & radio writer-performer, journalist, filmmaker and podcaster. She makes quirky little podcasts, cheeky docs and offbeat slots for Radio Television Hong Kong. She can currently be heard hosting 'Mental Ideas' and performing her monthly humour column 'Sharp Pains' on RTHK Radio 3. Her radio columns have also been published as goofy humour columns in the *South China Morning Post*'s *Sunday Post Magazine* and have formed the basis for short stories recently published in anthologies. Her first poem, 'War of Voices', won a place in the 2020 Proverse Poetry Prize anthology *Mingled Voices 5*. Sadie has made two documentaries, a series of podcasts, and co-produced a narrative feature film exploring mental health in unusual and imaginative ways. Her first 'Rant' column about the horror and dark humour of being labelled with a mental health condition that's often confused with the spectre of nuclear attack was published by the *South China Morning Post* in 2022. She runs two mental health non-profit groups and is an ambassador for mental health charity Mind HK. She has bipolar disorder and ADHD but hopes these are the two least interesting things about her. She believes that every time you laugh at yourself a tiny demon dies.

ZACHARY T. KNOX lives in the Des Moines Metropolitan, Iowa. His works have appeared in several small niche and underground publications.

GARY LAI lives in Hong Kong. He is the runner-up in the 2021 Mensa International Poetry Competition, with an entry entitled 'Magritte: A Reflection on the Pandemic.'

HO CHEUNG LEE Dr Ho-cheung (Peter) LEE is the founding editor of BALLOONS Lit. Journal and author of poetry chapbook *Something Celebrative or Immortal Under Another Birdless Sky* (Jamii Publishing). He was awarded Champion in two Hong Kong-based writing contests "the Oxford Primary English Writing Competition (2019) and Love Is All Around, the 2nd Hong Kong Chinese & English Essay-Writing Competition (2020), and a Gold Star prize in Creative Writing (Open Group) at the Singapore Performing Arts Festival (2021). His work (poetry/short stories/photography) has appeared in *Rattle*, *82 Review, *Shearsman Magazine*, Interpreters' House, Eunoia Review, *Typehouse Literary Magazine*, The Oddville Press, and elsewhere. His poetry was shortlisted in the Oxford Brookes University International Poetry Competition (2016), for erbacce-prize for poetry (2017), thrice for The Proverse Poetry Prize (2017, 2018 & 2020), and he was a finalist of the Real Good Poem Prize (2019). He teaches English in Hong Kong.

SHARON E. LUDAN holds a B.A. from the College of New Jersey and an M.S. from Boston University. As an American diplomat, Ludan has lived and worked in many countries throughout the world. Her work has been published by Proverse Hong Kong, Wingless Dreamer, Quillkeepers Press, Unleashed Press, the Kansai Scene, the OSIPP Journal, and elsewhere.

K. B. RYAN JOSHUA MAHINDAPALA, LLB, FRSA, is a Singaporean writer, author, and poet. His poem entitled, 'The Computer Has Decided! The Computer Has Decided!' was awarded a place in the Proverse Poetry Prize Anthology 2020, *Mingled Voices 5*. He is also the author of the critically acclaimed pulp noir crime fiction novella, *Spottisbrough* (Partridge Pub Singapore (October 2021).

CARMINA MASOLIVER is a poet from south London, and founder of She Grrrowls feminist arts nights. She has been sharing her poetry on both the page and the stage for over a decade, and her small chapbook was published by Nasty Little Press in 2014. Her latest book *Circles* is published by Burning Eye Books (2019) and is an illustrated long-form poem, and she recently self-published *Selected Poems: 2007 - 2012*, a mixed media pamphlet of poems. Her poetry has also been featured in publications such as *Popshot Magazine*, The Rialto and Brittle Star. Carmina was long-listed for the Young Poet Laureate for London award in 2013, the inaugural Jerwood Compton Poetry Fellowships in 2017, the Out-Spoken Prize in Performance Poetry in 2018 and 2022, and the Grindstone International Poetry Prize in 2020. Alumni of the Roundhouse Poetry Collective, she has featured at nights such as Bang Said the Gun, and festivals including Latitude, Bestival and Lovebox both as a collective and individually. She performed internationally whilst living abroad, in Singapore, and in Spain.

WAYNE PAUL MATTINGLY is a multi-award-winning playwright whose work has been staged in NYC; Westchester & Putnam Counties, N.Y; Los Angeles, San Francisco; Bangor, Maine; Denton & Houston, Texas; Chamblee, GA; Valdez, Alaska; Kauai, Hawaii; and London, England.

Winner of the 2007 Tennessee Chapbook Prize; 2011 Arts & Letters Prize in Drama, Finalist, Milledgeville, GA; 2012 Denton Community Theatre, Method and Madness

Competition & Festival, Third Prize, Denton, TX; 2012 The Last Frontier Theatre Conference,/Susan Nims Distinguished Play Playwright Award Finalist, Valdez, Alaska; 2012 Phoenix Theatre, Hormel New Play Festival Finalist; 2013 The Ashland New Plays Festival Semi-finalist, Ashland, OR; 2014 Ronald Duncan Literary Prize Finalist, United Kingdom; and 25th Annual International Playwriting Festival, Warehouse Theatre Co., London, U.K. and an IATC 2016 Cimientos Play Development Program Finalist, NYC.

He is proud to have been awarded a 2014 Helene Wurlitzer Foundation Fellowship Artists Residency Grant, Taos, NM; & to be a Grant Recipient of the 2014 & 2015 Disquiet International Literary Programs (Short Plays) in Lisbon, Portugal; and both a 2015/16 Can Serrat & 2017/18 Can Serrat International Artists Residency Grant Recipient, in Barcelona, Spain.

He was a founding member & Dramaturg of The Misfits Ensemble, L.A.: Founding Artistic Director of Tiger's Heart Players in N.Y: a Dramatist Guild, & Actors' Equity Association member. Last seen on stage in the 2013 Midtown International Theatre Festival in NYC, he was nominated for a Best Lead Actor Award. He has directed well over two dozen works in both CA & NY. His newest full-length drama, *Anthem*, was read at both The Village Playwrights in NYC & Axial Theatre in Ossining, NY. Published work can be found in *The Best 10-Minute Plays* (Smith & Kraus 2020, 2017), *More 10-Minute Plays for Teens* (Applause Theatre & Cinema Books, 2015), *Best Women's Monologues* (Smith & Kraus, 2014), *Poetry & Plays 14* (2007), *Best Women's Monologues & Best Stage Scenes* (Smith & Kraus, 1999).

JACK MAYER is a Vermont writer and pediatrician. His was the first pediatric practice in Eastern Franklin County, on the Canadian border, where he began writing essays, poems and short stories about his practice and hiking Vermont's Long Trail. He was a country doctor for ten years, often bartering medical care for eggs, firewood, and knitted afghans. From 1987 to 1991 Dr Mayer was a National Cancer Institute Fellow at Columbia University researching the molecular biology of cancer. Dr Mayer established Rainbow Pediatrics in Middlebury, Vermont in 1991 where he continues to practice primary care pediatrics. He is an Instructor in Pediatrics at the University of Vermont School of Medicine and an adjunct faculty for pre-medical students at Middlebury College. He was a participant at the Bread Loaf Writers' Conference in 2003 and 2005 (fiction) and 2008 (poetry). His first non-fiction book is *Life In A Jar: The Irena Sendler Project*. His new book, *Before The Court Of Heaven*, is historical fiction about the rise of Nazism, and has received 14 book awards. His collection of poems inspired and composed in wilderness, *Poems From The Wilderness*, was published in November 2020 and won the International Proverse Prize 2019.

LILY MAYO is studying literature in Boston, Massachusetts. Her writing has been featured in *The Dillydoun Review*, *Beyond Words Literary Magazine*, *Cathexis Northwest Press*, other literary magazines, and printed reading anthologies such as *Beyond Queer Words 2021*, *Realm Of Emotions* published by Poets Choice, the first print edition of *Sepia Quarterly*, and the 22nd edition of *Beyond Words International Literary Magazine* and more. She has a total of 15 publications and was awarded first runner-up in the Wingless Dreamer, "Ink The Universe", poetry competition.

TERRY MILLER is a Norfolk, England-based writer and sculptor. He honed his writing skills as a creative director for a number of advertising and creative agencies. Lately a successful game inventor, Terry utilizes his skills to create evocative, funny, and sometimes disturbing poetry.
Written in an accessible form, Terry's poetry is deceptively complex, often tackling topical issues and exploring deep emotional issues. Terry's poems have been featured in several international poetry anthologies and sculptures in several exhibitions. His work has been recently published in the following collections: *It's Not Easy, Nursery Rhymes and Stories from Around the World, Found Proverbs, PS It's Still Poetry, Winter, Poems that make you Laugh*.

KEITH NUNES (Aotearoa/New Zealand) was nominated for Best Small Fictions and the Pushcart Prize, and he won the 2017 Flash Frontier Short Fiction Award. He has had poetry, fiction, haiku and visuals published around the globe.

DENISE O'HAGAN is a Sydney-based editor and poet, married with two sons. She grew up in Italy, which might have had something to do with her falling in love with lyric poetry, and studied in the UK where she completed her Masters. She has a background as an editor in commercial book publishing in London and Sydney. Recipient of the Dalkey Poetry Prize and former poetry editor for Irish literary journal *The Blue Nib*, her work is widely published both in Australia and overseas, including in *Quadrant*, *The Copperfield Review* and *Books Ireland*.

HELEN OLIVER is an ex-ESL teacher, a materials writer and editor. Having taught at the British Council, Hong Kong, from 1978-1980, she then lived and taught in Japan for 15 years, before returning to work in New Zealand. Part-time work now allows more time for tai chi, music, books and poetry, family and friends. She lives by the sea, and spends time kayaking, volunteering for seashore bird protection, and wandering the beaches of the Coromandel. She has had poems published in *Mingled Voices 4*, 2019, *Mingled Voices 5*, 2020, *Mingled Voices 6*, 2021 (including a 3rd prize place) and *Stay Well Here* a NZPS Poetry Anthology 2020.

RENA ONG is an English lady, who lives with her husband in Singapore. They have a son who lives abroad. She enjoys immersing herself in various creative areas and delights in others creative talents. She enjoys the quietness and reflective time of poetry writing as well as its playfulness.

JUN PAN (Janice) lives in Hong Kong and works as an associate professor in the Department of Translation, Interpreting and Intercultural Studies at Hong Kong Baptist University. She is an interpreter, researcher, and poet. Jun's childhood dream was to become a writer, film director or painter. With a passion for reading and writing, she founded a Chinese poetry club and started publishing Chinese poems (shi and ci) at age twelve in her birthplace of Xiangtan, Hunan. She then studied English language and literature in Jiangsu and interpreting in Shanghai. After becoming an interpreter, she came to Hong Kong in 2008 for her PhD in interpreting studies and has been teaching interpreting and translation at local tertiary institutions since then. She continues writing whenever possible. Jun has found her childhood immersion in literature and culture important and invaluable in her life and career. Apart from introducing Chinese culture to many of her clients when she worked as an interpreter, Jun also participated in the translation of several classic works from English to Chinese, including John Ruskin's five-volume *Modern Painters*.

JOANNA RADWANSKA-WILLIAMS was born in Warsaw, Poland, and spent a part of her childhood in London, England. She received her B.A. with a double major in English and Linguistics (awarded with Highest Honors) and her Ph.D. in Linguistics from the University of North Carolina at Chapel Hill, USA. Her dissertation was published as *A Paradigm Lost: The Linguistic Theory of Miko'aj Kruszewski* (Amsterdam: John Benjamins, 1993). She taught Slavic Linguistics (Polish and Russian) at the State University of New York at Stony Brook (1989-1994) and the University of Illinois at Chicago (1994-1995), and English Linguistics at Nanjing University (1996-1999) and the Chinese University of Hong Kong (1999-2003). In 2003, she joined Macao Polytechnic Institute, where she is now a full professor in the School of Languages and Translation.

Joanna's poetry has been anthologized in several collections, including *Lingua Franca: An Anthology of Poetry by Linguists* (edited by Donna Jo Napoli and Emily Norwood Rando; Lake Bluff, Illinois: Jupiter Press, 1989), *Montage of Life* (Owings Mills, Maryland: The National Library of Poetry, 1998), *I Roll the Dice: Contemporary Macao Poetry* (edited by Christopher Kit Kelen and Agnes Vong; Macao: Association of Stories in Macao, 2008), *Lotus Field 2018: Reflections* (edited by Zi-yu Lin, Joanna Radwanska-Williams and Yunfeng Zhang; Macao: Macao Polytechnic Institute, 2018), Songs for Salamanders (edited by Cat Dossett; Boston: Pen & Anvil Press, 2020); *Mingled Voices 2: International Proverse Poetry Prize Anthology 2017*, *Mingled Voices 3: International Proverse Poetry Prize Anthology 2018*, *Mingled Voices 4: International Proverse Poetry Prize Anthology 2019* , *Mingled Voices 5: International Proverse Poetry Prize Anthology 2020* (edited by Gillian Bickley and Verner Bickley; Hong Kong: Proverse Hong Kong, 2018, 2019, 2020, 2021), and *Mingled Voices 6: International Proverse Poetry Prize Anthology 2021*, in which she was awarded 1st Prize for her poem 'Confucius Temple in Qufu'.

KERRY RAWLINSON is a mental nomad. She left Zambia decades ago to explore, landing in Canada. Fast forward: she pursues art and literature's muses around the Okanagan, still barefoot, tiptoeing between dislocation & belonging. Awards: winner of the Glittery Literary Flash Contest; Edinburgh International Flash; finalist in Room, Princemere and Palette Emerging Poet Prizes. Recent work: Prism Review; O:JA&L; Grain; Epoch; Event Poetry; Prairie Fire; Sarasvati; Unlost Journal; Cagibi; Carousel; Queen Mob's Teahouse; amongst others. When not testing established constructs, kerry kayaks with her husband.

M. ANN REED teaches the Organic Unity Study of Literature to support the Deep Ecology Movement globally and locally. Her doctoral research considers literature a spiritual and medical art, met by the privilege of teaching and learning in like-minded Eastern European and Asian countries. Her poems support various literary arts journals: *Antithesis*, *Azure*, Burningword, Eastern Iowa Review, Parabola, Proverse, Hong Kong, Psychological Perspectives and The Poeming Pigeon. Finishing Line Press published her chapbook, making oxygen, remaining inside this pure hollow note. Her book-length non-fiction, *Strange Kindness*, co-authored with Mabel S. Chu Tow was initially published by University Press of America, now offered by Rowman & Littlefield.

VINNI C. RELWANI lives in Singapore, calling it home for the last 25 years, with a soft-spot for Hong Kong where she was born and raised. A homemaker and mum, Vinni enjoys writing poetry and short stories, a few of which have found their way into the Proverse Poetry publishing realm.

ALLEGRA JOSTAD SILBERSTEIN grew up on a farm in Wisconsin but has lived in California since 1963. Her love of poetry began as a child when her mother would recite poems as she worked. Now that she is retired there is more time for singing and dancing as well as poetry. She has three chapbooks of poetry. In the spring of 2015, Cold River Press published her first book and she is widely published in journals such as *Blue Unicorn, California Quarterly, Iodine Poetry* and *Poetry Now*. In March of 2010 she was honored to become the first Poet Laureate for the city of Davis, CA.

WESLEY D. SIMS has published three chapbooks of poetry: *When Night Comes* (Finishing Line Press, Georgetown, Kentucky, 2013); *Taste of Change* (Iris Press, Oak Ridge, TN, 2019); and *A Pocketful of Little Poems* (Amazon, 2020). His work has appeared in *Artemis Journal, Bewildering Stories, Connecticut Review, G.W. Review, Liquid Imagination, Pine Mountain Sand and Gravel, Plum Tree Tavern, Novelty Magazine, Poem, Poetry Quarterly, Time of Singing, The South Carolina Review*, and several other journals and anthologies.

HAYLEY ANN SOLOMON is a New Zealand author and poet. She is a two-time winner of a Proverse International publication Prize: in 2016 for her debut anthology of poetry, *Celestial Promise,* and in 2018 for her collection of short stories entitled *Under the shade of the feijoa tree*. She is published primarily by Kensington (USA) Proverse (Hong Kong) and Calumet (USA) and was a 2021 semi-finalist for the 2020 Proverse Prize. Her work has featured in literary journals and best short story anthologies that range from Compose, Rose and Thorn,, Page and Blackmore, the Momaya Press Annual Reviews and the US Binnacle. She was twice listed in the top ten for Momaya Press and has three times been an Honoree of the University of Maine at Machias. She has a Masters degree in Librarianship and Information Studies from the University of Victoria, Wellington, and worked as the Head of Distance Services for the University of Otago Library. She sings chorally as a first soprano and has a firm belief in the value of kindness in the world.

ABBIE JOHNSON TAYLOR is the author of three novels, two poetry collections, and a memoir. Her work has appeared in *The Weekly Avocet, Magnets and Ladders,* and other publications.

LUISA TERNAU was born and raised in Trieste, Northeastern Italy. After graduating at the University of Trieste she moved to the UK (London and one year in Wales). She obtained an MA in English Literature at King's College, University of London. Since then Luisa has lived in a number of countries across three continents. She has been based in Hong Kong for the last ten years. Luisa likes to write poems and short stories. Her inspiration is life in its multiple facets. She is interested in literature, ranging from poetry to folk tales, from all over the world and from every era. Luisa won a third prize in the inaugural Proverse Poetry Prize competition and her poems have appeared in each of the Proverse Poetry Prize *Mingled Voices* Anthologies.

EDWARD A. TIESSE recently returned to Washington State after living for several years in the Chicago area. From his home on clear days, he can see Mount Baker and the Canadian Cascades. Living so close to Canada makes it easy to slip across the border when it becomes necessary.

Edward A. Tiesse has many interests. He loves to cook and recently began baking bread which he soon learned is much like writing poetry. That is, the combinations of flour, water and yeast have many variables and so baking is much like trying to find the right word and its place in a line. Edward's poetry has been published in *The Front Porch Review*, *The Sea Letter*, *Whatcom Writes* and in the Proverse Poetry Prize Anthologies, *Mingled Voices*.

ROGER UREN has had an extensive career in diplomacy, media work and literature. He has written a number of books on Asia-related historical events and culture.

ANNA VERHAEGH lives in Wellington New Zealand. As an immigrant from The Netherlands in May 2000, she has since then become familiar with the English language and the thrill of writing. She was home-schooled and graduated from the University of Waikato in 2021. In her spare time she enjoys Scottish Country dancing and crafts and is actively involved with the local Girl Guide Unit as a leader.

KEWAYNE WADLEY is a 34-year-old American poet who is known for his innovative—sometimes sultry— approach to his ideologies on love. He currently lives in Memphis Tennessee and has a deep passion for music. Currently he has been published in 15 anthologies & has a small collection of his own under his belt with another one that he hopes to release soon

ANSON HONGHUA WANG, PhD, is an Assistant Professor in Translation. Her research interests are interpreter and translator training, gender and translation and second language acquisition. She is a practicing translator and interpreter. Besides research, she has a wide range of interests including reading, watching movies and hiking. She is the vice president of the Hong Kong Association of University Women and associate secretary of Hong Kong Translation Society. She is also a member of International Association for Translation and Intercultural Studies.

GEORGE WATT is a past contributor to four volumes in the *Mingled Voices* series. He had previously published in the areas of academic criticism and English pedagogy. Lately he has been more interested in purely creative enterprise. *Sandpaper Swimming*, a collection of poetry on explorers Burke and Wills and their tragic deaths in the 1860s, was published by Flying Island Books in 2019. *The Finley Confession*, a novel, was the winner of the 2020 International Proverse Prize for a previously unpublished full-length work. His academic appointments include Professor of English and Dean of the Faculty of Foreign Languages at Nagoya Shoka Daigaku in Japan, and founding Master of HFPJC, one of the constituent colleges in the University of Macau. He was professor of Comparative Culture at the new Hokkaido Campus of Komazawa University in Japan, and was head of two residential colleges at the Australian National University. He has also held visiting posts in the USA and Singapore.

MICHAEL WITTS has been writing and publishing poetry for more than forty years. He has three published collections are; *Sirens* (Island Press), *SOUTH* (Makar Press) and *DUMB MUSIC* (Fling Poetry).. He was a founding editor of *Dodo Magazine*. He lives, works and writes in Australia.

THE EDITORS

VERNER BICKLEY was born in the North-West of England, and educated there, in Wales and London, and has lived in Asian and Pacific countries for over fifty years.

He has been scholar, teacher, manager, broadcaster, stage and film actor and cultural diplomat in a life often enlivened by music and song, dance and entertainment.

Verner's many scholarly articles and book publications are mainly on educational and cross-cultural topics. He has however also published two volumes of memoirs: *Footfalls Echo in the Memory* and *Steps To Paradise And Beyond*. His five-book graded poetry anthology, *Poems to Enjoy*, has been popular since the 1960s. These now benefit from accompanying recordings of all poems in the texts (read mostly by himself, but some by his wife, Gillian), as well as from teaching and performance notes. He is a member of the United Kingdom Society of Authors.

With his wife, Gillian, Verner Bickley is joint-publisher of Proverse Hong Kong and co-founder of the Proverse Prize and the Proverse Poetry Prize.

Verner was a naval officer in pre-independent Sri Lanka and India. He served in the Colonial Education Service in Singapore and, later, as a British Council officer in post-independence Burma, in Indonesia and Japan. In Hawaii from 1971 to 1981, he served as the Director and for a period Chairman of Directors of the Culture Learning Institute at the East-West Center, established by the US Congress in Hawaii in 1960 and functioning as a US-based institution for public diplomacy with international governance, staffing, students and Fellows.

From 1972 to 1980, Verner led a small team of anthropologists, cross-cultural psychologists and linguists, focusing on the different ways in which individuals and whole societies cope in bicultural and multicultural contexts and how they address problems presented by different cultural norms. Among many interesting projects, his Institute provided for the pioneering voyage of the canoe, *Hōküle'a*, from Hawaii to Tahiti, disproving the theories of Thor Heyerdahl.

Verner was instrumental in bringing to conferences in Honolulu writers who included Guy Amirthanayagam, Leon

Edel, Vincent Eri, Nissim Ezekial, Reuel Denney, Janet Frame, Allen Ginsberg, Syd Harrex, Thomas Keneally, Maxine Hong-Kingston, Arun Kolatkhar, Ananda Murthy, Kenzaburo Oe, Kushwant Singh, Kamala Markandaya, R.K. Narayan, A.K. Ramanajuan, E.R. Sarachchandra, Wole Soyinka and Albert Wendt.

After leaving Hawaii, and while in Saudia Arabia for a two-year assignment with the national airline, Saudia, Verner was responsible for a multi-national staff of 100 persons, mainly, but not exclusively, in Jeddah and Riyadh.

In 1983, Verner was appointed founding director of the Institute of Language in Education in Hong Kong and held that post until 1992. During that period, he created and led annual International conferences on Applied Linguistics and founded and directed the journal, the ILEJ.

Refusing to retire, Verner continues to live in Hong Kong where he writes and publishes on a variety of topics. He was founding Chairman of the English-Speaking Union (Hong Kong) and continued as Chairman of the Executive Committee for sixteen years. He recently passed this responsibility over to a new chairman, but in his capacity as Chairman Emeritus continues with his own portfolio of tasks. As Chairman, he traveled for many years to the Mainland of China to join other judges of the national Public-Speaking Competition organised by national media. He was an adjudicator for the Hong Kong Schools Music and Speech Association's annual Speech Festival for many years and for a while was Representative in Hong Kong for Trinity College London.

Verner Bickley's experiences have created in him an interest in cross-cultural experiences and attitudes and in a desire to communicate what he has learnt. Through his memoirs as well as his personal contacts, he hopes not only to interest others, but to encourage them to build on their own desire to learn about and empathise with other cultures.

THE EDITORS

GILLIAN BICKLEY, born and educated in the United Kingdom, has lived mostly in Hong Kong since 1970. She has been a member of the Society of Authors in the United Kingdom since her school days.

Her poetry collections include *For the Record and other Poems of Hong Kong, Moving House and other Poems from Hong Kong, Sightings: a collection of poetry*, *China Suite and other Poems, Perceptions*, and *Grandfather's Robin*. Selections from these collections have been published bilingually: in the English-Romanian *Poems/Poeme* (Romanian translation by Carolina Ilica and Dumitru M. Ion) and the English-Italian, *Avvistamenti, pensieri e sentimenti* (Italian translation by Luisa Ternau). Two collections— *Moving House* and *For the Record*— have also been published in Chinese; individual poems have been published in Arabic, Catalan, Chinese, Czech, French, German, Romanian, Turkish and other languages. *Over the Years* (2017) is a selection from her previously published work, selected by Verner Bickley. In 2014, she was awarded the "Grand Prix Orient-Occident Des Arts" at the 18th International Festival, "Curtea de Argeş Poetry Nights", held in Romania. Gillian Bickley is one of the Hong Kong poets discussed in Agnes S. L. Lam's study, *Becoming poets: The Asian English Experience*.

Gillian has written or edited several non-fiction books in different fields: *The Golden Needle: The Biography of Frederick Stewart, 1836-1889 (founder of Hong Kong Government Education)*, Hong Kong Baptist University and David C. Lam Institute for East-West Studies, 1997; *Hong Kong Invaded! A '97 Nightmare*, University of Hong Kong Press, Hong Kong, 2001; *The Development of Education in Hong Kong, 1841-1897: as revealed through the Early Education Reports of the Hong Kong Government, 1848-1896*, Proverse Hong Kong, Hong Kong, 2002; *The Stewarts of Bourtreebush*, Centre for Scottish Studies, University of Aberdeen, Scotland, 2003; *A Magistrate's Court in 19th Century Hong Kong: Court in Time*, Proverse Hong Kong, first edition, 2005; second edition, 2009; *The Complete Court Cases of Magistrate Frederick Stewart*, Proverse Hong Kong, 2008; *In Time of War* (in collaboration with Richard Collingwood-

Selby), an edition based on the writings of Henry C.S. Collingwood-Selby (1898-1992), Lieutenant Commander in the Royal Navy, Proverse Hong Kong, 2013, *Through American Eyes: The Journals of George Washington (Farley) Heard (1837-1875)*, Proverse Hong Kong, 2017; *Journeys with a Mission: Travel Journals of The Right Revd George Smith (1815-1871), first Bishop of Victoria, Hong Kong (1849-1865)*, Proverse Hong Kong, 2018.

Five of these fourteen English-language books received publication support from Hong Kong Arts Development Council (HKADC) and four from the Lord Wilson Heritage Trust. The extensive research necessary for seven of the non-fiction works listed was made possible by research grants awarded by the Hong Kong Baptist University and one was supported by a private sponsor.

Dr Bickley was Senior Lecturer / Associate Professor in the Department of English at the Hong Kong Baptist University for twenty-two years. She has been a full-time faculty member at the University of Lagos, Nigeria; the University of Auckland, New Zealand; and at the University of Hong Kong.

For several years, Gillian was an adjudicator at the world-famous Hong Kong Schools Music & Speech Association's annual Speech Festival and has also been a judge for the Budding Poets' Society Hong Kong.

More recently, as co-ordinator of literary activities for the English-Speaking Union Hong Kong, a non-profit registered educational charity, she has led reading appreciation sessions which are open to the community and assists to deliver reading courses at local schools. She has worked with the Gifted Education Section of the Education Bureau to encourage creative writing among students. On a freelance basis, she has taught creative reading / writing courses at the Hong Kong Academy for Gifted Education (HKAGE) and at the University of Hong Kong School for Professional and Continuing Education (HKU SPACE) and been a guest lecturer on poetry at Lingnan University Community College. Her creative reading / writing course at HKU SPACE continues to be offered. In 2016, she managed twenty and hosted seventeen meet-the-author events at a Hong Kong bookshop. On occasion, she accepts invitations to speak at school Reading Festivals and similar.

Following her career in academia, Gillian has become an experienced publisher, project-manager, text editor, and production manager, including of poetry, non-fiction, fiction and academic writing. She has been President of the Hong Kong Association of University Women and has recently stepped aside from her role as Council Member and a Vice-President of the Royal Asiatic Society (Hong Kong).

PROVERSE HONG KONG: AN INTRODUCTION

Together, Gillian and Verner Bickley are the publishers of Proverse Hong Kong, a Hong Kong-based press which publishes both local and international authors, including non-native users of English. They are also co-founders of two annual international literary prizes for work submitted in English: in 2008, they founded the Proverse Prize for unpublished book-length fiction, non-fiction or poetry, and, in 2016, they established the Proverse Poetry Prize (for single poems which may have been previously published in a language other than English). In the case of both prizes, entries are received from around the world.

Beginning in 2007 up to December 2021, Proverse has managed, edited and published about 139 English-language books by Hong Kong and international writers, five Chinese-language books, one English / Chinese and one English / Italian bilingual book. Of the English-language books, about twenty-eight have been awarded publication support by Hong Kong Arts Development Council (HKADC), four by Lord Wilson Heritage Trust and two by the Ride Fund for publication in the Royal Asiatic Society Hong Kong Studies series. One received a publication grant from the Ministry of Culture of the Czech Republic and one received a publication grant from the Ministry of Culture and Tourism of the Republic of Turkey.

Twice a year, from 2009, Proverse organises literary events in Hong Kong, open to the public. New books are launched, writers are introduced and launching authors give brief talks. Announcements are made relating to the current year's Proverse Prize for unpublished fiction, non-fiction or poetry, and the Proverse Poetry Prize (for single short poems); prizes are presented to those winning authors who are present. Edited videos of some of these events are available at the Proverse youtube channel, and photos of most of them are available on the Proverse website, proversepublishing.com.

Gillian and Verner work hard to bring authors before the reading public and to encourage reading as well as writing. On four occasions, they have administered Reading Development Grants awarded by the Hong Kong Arts Development Council. In 2016, as implementation of one of these, they arranged twenty meet-the-author sessions, held at a

Hong Kong bookshop. To reach an international audience, edited videos of these talks are available on Youtube.

Of the titles published by Proverse, several have attracted a Preface or advance appreciation from figures of international reputation, most notably perhaps, from Václav Havel (for the English translation of Olga Walló's *Tightrope: A Bohemian Tale*).

Two titles (Peter Gregoire's, *Article 109* and *The Devil You Know*) were best sellers at Dymocks Hong Kong.

The publication by Proverse of the late Sophronia Liu's book, *A Shimmering Sea*, was a major argument in the award to Sophronia of a posthumous PhD at the University of Minnesota.

Other writers published by Proverse have also benefited in their literary careers, a couple of them taking a leadership role in local literary groups.

Gillian's and Verner's own books and all those by other authors published by Proverse, are available internationally as well as locally, including through the Chinese University of Hong Kong Press. There are copies in the British Library and other legal deposit libraries in the United Kingdom, and in the Hong Kong Public Library system, as well as in many university and public libraries world-wide. Books by Australian writers have been deposited in the National Library of Australia and similar deposits are ongoing in other countries.

Further information

Gillian Bickley, 'The Proverse Prize, *Journal of Postcolonial Writing*, Vol 59, 2023 Issue 1.
https://www.tandfonline.com/eprint/TKVG8HZSZWX6R4CUJUKM/full?target=10.1080/17449855.2022.2101653

Proverse titles page: https://cup.cuhk.edu.hk/Proversehk

Proverse Autumn Reception 2022 video (2nd edit): https://youtu.be/j4gCaga6hUQ)

Proverse Youtube channel:
youtube.com/@ProversePublishing),

[1] **Stroke**. Vinita Agrawal writes, "The poem is for my father. He suffered a stroke in 2015 and went into a coma and had to be put on a ventilator for more than three weeks. He passed away on the 27th day of his coma, waking up only twice to make eye contact with me."

[2] **A wish for my old age**. Shikha Bansal writes that her poem, "is an exploration of the freedoms that come or should come with old age. We cannot control the passage of time, but perhaps we could control to some degree, if we are lucky, how we live out the final years of our lives."

[3] **Once Again: The Courage of Everyday Life.** Alan Bern writes that his poem, "grew out of my over fifteen years of working with disabled library patrons as the Disability Services Librarian at the Berkeley (California) Public Library. To say that I learned a lot from this work would be a vast understatement. Many of our disabled community members are heroic in their energy and work to meet the challenges in daily life. This goes almost without saying though many of these same community members perhaps do not even think that way. They just persist and have jobs and relationships and meet challenges as they can. In any case the passing of the Americans with Disabilities Act (ADA) in 1990 in the United States was both overdue and revolutionary at the same moment. And it gave many new challenges to everyone and certainly to libraries: physical spaces needed to be made accessible often in quite complex ways, but there were many other accommodations that needed to take place, some entirely unpredictable to us all. Finding the epigraph from our great leader and orator Martin Luther King, Jr., completed the poem for me since it put this heroism in a larger and more communitarian context. I also felt it important to begin the poem with an experience that many of us have had: seeing disabled people and being uncomfortable or amazed or another unusual response. Having also worked for years with children

in the library, I learned from them that one could be interested, but also compassionate and inclusive. Of course, some children are rude in their staring, but rest assured, so are many adults. And what of the miracle, is this a prejudicial response? I don't think so: I believe that it is a miracle that any of us function and survive. So, miracle? Certainly."

[4] **Out of the Blue Sea of Letters**. Maria Elena Blanco writes, "In this poem there is a parallelism and an imbrication of the 'story' with the act of writing which involve the two elements of the title: 'Out of the blue' and 'sea of letters' suggest this dual relationship.

The poem refers to someone ('my father') who is swimming and will eventually come out of the water ('the sea'), but at the end of the poem (that is, at the end of the act of writing) he not only comes out of the water but suddenly ('out of the blue') is seen as coming out of the poem itself among the last written letters ('the sea of letters'), with the same suddenness and surprise effect inherent to the act of writing itself.

The impulse to write the poem and its *dénouement* both come as a surprise, a combination of an inner pulsion and unforeseeable chance. Between that beginning and that end, what is usually called the 'story' develops: a mention of a seaside venue ('Celimar') where the swimming takes place; the physical description of that place and of the father; the suggestion of other 'characters' ('we', 'grandfather') and of certain other past events; the main lyric persona's remembrances and feelings; the return, many years later, to that same place—now empty and forlorn—where someone who said she couldn't swim is about to jump into the water...

But something happens/someone emerges 'out of the blue' from 'the sea of letters'. The appearance of the father propitiates and concludes the act of writing and both—character and writing—save the lyric persona and the 'story' from their symbolic death (that is, from not being able to tell / not being told), while actually making the poem whole.

As it is frequent in my poetry, the 'story' has as much to do with the act of writing as with a 'theme' or 'content': form and content here become one."

[5] **I Dreamt I Was on The Yangtze River**. Gavin Bourke writes, "I wrote this poem about a recent dream I experienced."

[6] **My Rare Chinese Winding-Clock**. Gavin Bourke writes, "This is a poem I wrote about a Chinese clock I bought in a Dublin Market about a year ago and my ambitious plans to restore it."

[7] **Any Thing**. Lawrence Bridges writes, "This poem contains flashes of memory of living in New York in a dreamscape of particular images and behaviours like, 'I follow the souls up Twenty-First Street, subway, sinking with trotting heads, all with wet hair.'"
"The comma at the end of Street is an ungrammatical time compression, like jump cuts in film. I'm trying to compress the diurnal journey down the stair and into the subway to target the visual 'all with wet hair' (after rain, after morning showers, etc). Wet hair is one of the 'things' of anything, like the 'elegant garden of bedside tools', triggers of beauty per the last line of the poem. Likewise, 'The strap hung loose and the watch tightened on the wrist' is a visual and a 'thing' that crashes the poet from thought into beauty. In New York subways, straps, long since replaced with poles for rider steadying, are visual features on subways every New Yorker knows. People from New Jersey are pejoratively referred to as 'strap hangers'. Ostensibly the poet glances at his watch on his left wrist, further triggering the epiphany. In the poem, the italicized phrase functions as a faux quotation and a deceptive cadence at the entrance of the poem, signified by the semi-colon."

[8] **The Foam of the Days**. Lina Buividaviciute writes that this poem was inspired by Boris Vian's novel, *Froth on the Daydream*.

[9] **Five photos of Diana**. Sean Camshon explains that this was, "Written to a woman I met online who lives half a world away. She has sent me five photos of herself over the last three months, and she was waiting to hear from me, so I wanted to say I wait as well."

[10] **Resurrection**. Carol Flake Chapman writes, "I have used the myth of Isis and Osiris to describe the annual resurrection or renewal in nature that happens every spring, despite our frequent doubts that spring will ever come."

[11] **Paper Crane**. Tom Choi writes, "Folding a paper crane (origami) can be a profoundly transforming deed by those who stubbornly seek the good in life and are willing to share it with others."

[12] **Railway Station When the Doors Open**. Tom Choi explains that this is, "An inspired snapshot of people heading to work in the morning at an MTR station (Sheung Wan, Central Business District) in Hong Kong." He also explains that, "the name 'La Prosperité' was meant to be an unspecified/fictional painting (in French so as to hint at some sense of impressionism). Since it was set forth as a rhetorical question, I think there is no definite person to attribute the painting to. The ending question was mainly a device to invite the reader to think about what kind of mechanisms/material conditions (urban, if not limited to HK) prosperity is predicated on. In all likelihood, it's a coincidence that there is already a film with that title; the poem has no connection with the film."

[13] **Haven Among Trees**. Suzanne Cottrell writes, "Thirty-five years ago, my husband and I built a house on a cleared field surrounded by woods in the central region of North Carolina. We enjoy the serenity and solitude of Granville County. Hiking in the woods is calming and restorative. Recently, I've been reading about the communication among plants, particularly trees. When trees are in distress, especially from drought, tiny air bubbles form and the tubes for transporting fluids within their trunks collapse. Trees make a variety of sounds depending on the cause: insects, drought, fire, wind, and temperature changes.

I've been alarmed by the number of county residents who are clear-cutting the trees on their property and are not reseeding. Not only are animal habitats reduced, but the land suffers from increased erosion and run-off. Through my writing, I'm endeavoring to raise awareness and advocate for forest protection and reforestation.

Notes

The <u>bitternut hickory tree</u> is native to North Carolina and much of the eastern United States. The height of the deciduous shade tree is about 80 feet or 24 meters, and the trunk width is up to 50 feet or about 15 meters. The bark is gray or light brown. Although the nuts are edible, they have a bitter taste.

The <u>wood thrush</u> is a song bird with reddish-brown feathers and black spots on a white breast and pot belly. The wood thrush perches on high tree branches and sings at dawn and at dusk.

A <u>mantra</u> is a repeated sound or phrase often used for inspiration, meditation, or prayer.

[14] **Body Full of Heatstroke**. Julio Diaz writes, While the poem is mainly in English, it does include a few Spanish words such as "desierto" (desert), its diminutive version "desiertito" (tiny/baby desert), "pa' lo santitos" (for the tiny/baby saint), and "mira sol" (look [the] sun). This poem is an overhaul of itself such that it mimicked the feelings of desire and change that I experienced in the midst of re/writing the poem.""

[15] **7 miles high**. Neil Douglas writes that this, "is a found poem. Found poetry reframes existing texts into poetic form lending the text fresh insight or new meaning. This poem was written during a course themed around birds."

[16] **Bruce Lee in a yellow tracksuit**. Neil Douglas writes that his poem, "is inspired by an exhibition I attended at Hong Kong Heritage Museum titled 'Bruce Lee: Kung Fu. Art. Life.'

It is written as a duplex - a form innovated by American poet Jericho Brown which has been eloquently described by him as a combination of sonnet, ghazal and blues. When first writing in this form he spoke of the need he felt to subvert the sonnet.

The sonnet arose originally from the Italian court as a 14-line lyric form often expressing romantic feelings. The Shakespearean sonnet that we are familiar with took this further with a structure and musicality that offers a compressed memorable message while balancing lyric with narrative progression. The Ghazal is a 7th century Arabic form, often with a romantic theme, written in couplets and employing repeated or rhyming words or phrases. It often deals with its themes in a metaphysical sense. The blues is an African-American musical form which is traditionally reflective and melancholic using weighted sonic couplets in a characteristic call and response style.

My poem has 14 lines and employs some call and response couplets using repetition of the end word in the second line of a couplet in the first line of the following couplet. This allows continuity of thought with dynamic progression but also allows circularity by arriving back at the title/first line at the conclusion of the poem. This circularity is important as a recognition of Bruce Lee's philosophy and to envelope the complementary contrasts in the poem - thought/feeling, tenderness/compulsion, sun/moon.
The emotional lyric in the poem arises from Bruce Lee having a meditative dialogue with himself. I like to think of it as a love song to our universe."

[17] **Geography Teacher**. Neil Douglas writes that this, "is an eco-poem inspired by studying Geography at a state school in the United Kingdom during the 1970s."

[18] **Mr Milano**. Neil Douglas writes, "The Italian in this poem translates into various forms of 'let's dance'."

[19] **Sarah Van Fleet Come Dawn**. Casey Hampton writes, "Not sure this matters, but this is an example of nesting poetry.— This is the practice of combining multiple poems of the same form, sharing a common theme, into a single poem, while honoring the original form, in this case, the Haiku."

[20] **Imagine Nation**. Sadie Kaye explains, "This piece emerged from an essay I wrote in group training to be an ambassador for

the Hong Kong mental health charity Mind HK. I have bipolar disorder and I was trying to explain how a hallucination feels. When I performed it to the group, they commented that they thought it was poetic and encouraged me to develop it as a poem. Or maybe they were deluded? (Most of them had mental health issues, too!) I don't know if it qualifies as a poem or a poetic piece of prose. But it comes straight from the heart and I hope you enjoy reading it."

[21] **Tidal Slave.** Sadie Kaye writes, 'Tidal Slave' is set in a dystopian Hong Kong at an unspecified time in the future; a Hong Kong that has experienced some form of climate-change-related natural disaster in which the sea reclaimed most of the land Hong Kong had 'stolen' from it in land reclamation projects and wreaked revenge by swallowing it. In fact, the whole poem is intended as a lucid dream, hallucination or delusion of the bipolar protagonist, not as a response to real-world events. It is an emotional response to grief and loss of a loved one, panic about the length and sense of stringent Zero Covid measures, fears about the environment, war and geopolitical instability and how all this has impacted my own mental health and the mental health of others around me.

Bipolar is a tidal mental illness that mirrors the sea. It is characterised by periods of impulsivity, restlessness, delusions and creativity, followed by periods of despair that can lead to intrusive suicidal thoughts. 'Lying flat' is a popular Chinese term for doing the bare minimum to survive. It can be viewed positively as a period of calm reflection where intuition has space to breathe and better life choices can be made in the future. But it can also be viewed negatively as a sign of hopelessness that your voice will not be heard and the choices you make will not have any impact on shaping your future. Lying flat in this poem is a metaphor for the depressed cycle of bipolar disorder. The drowning represents the intrusive suicidal thoughts that accompany depressive episodes, even if there is no intention of committing suicide. Even though the poem ends on a dark note, it also signifies renewal. The tide keeps turning and so does the opportunity to replace something that has been destroyed with something better.

²² **youth's decadence**. Zachary Knox writes, "My poem can be summarized by my juvenile belief system internal collapse when confronted with the compounding accumulation of real-life events shaking my overall foundation and sense of being."

²³ **A Good Day**. Ho Cheung Lee writes, "This quatrain poem is written with iambic trimeter. It is considerably lengthier than the suggested 30 lines and yet, hopefully, its accessibility makes up for that. This verse depicts an unattended child at home making a video to kill time during the pandemic period. His day seems to be uneventful, and while we pity him for being affected by the unstable world, this routineness may already be a blessing compared to the lives of those severely jeopardized by the plague and war."

²⁴ **Machu Picchu**. Ho Cheung Lee writes, "Teaching a lesson has become unpredictable with the 'interference' of modern technology. This verse depicts a classic example of how I handled and felt about a lesson more or less disturbed by the need to use certain devices."

²⁵ **Moonlight**. Ho Cheung Lee writes, "I bought an old banknote from an antique store. I was very contented with it till I discovered a hidden flaw. Yet, this flaw provoked me in a poetic way.
<u>Note</u>: the "Ngo" in italics (stanza 8) was the intrusive sound I heard from a guy's singing."

²⁶ **Replay**. Ho Cheung Lee writes, "This verse truthfully depicts what I saw as I read past messages from my family's WhatsApp group, from happy messages to sad news. It is always amazing how life could be so effectively summed up electronically and revisited via your fingertip."

²⁷ **And the Universe Responds**. Sharon Ludan writes, "This poem is the sequel to 'To the Universe', which originally appeared in *Mingled Voices 5*. Together the two poems form a dialogue between the speaker and the universe. In the first poem, the speaker addresses the universe, lamenting her current state of ambiguity and indecision about the future. It's

about reaching a certain stage in life, a crossroads, the end of one chapter and beginning of the next...although one doesn't quite know what the next episode will be, so one must just step to the edge of the known and leap into the unknown. 'Must I still be brave?' the persona wails... 'To the very end?' 'And the Universe Responds' continues the dialogue with the universe's response."

[28] **A wasteland of arrows**. K B Ryan Joshua Mahindapala writes, "This poem describes the detrimental effects of climate change on our mental and physical well-being. It presents a post-apocalyptic scenario where the planet is on the brink of extinction. The end of humanity as we know it can be attributed to the corrupt and boastful who prey on those who are weak to feed their own ego and fill their own pockets, without sparing a thought for the greater good or the health of the planet and of every living species that inhabits this place called Earth.
Centuries of evolution, scientific discovery and the burgeoning of the arts and culture, represented by the arrow, which symbolises forward movement and progress, lie to rot in a wasteland because of a greedy few who mock us all and use words to tell lies instead of doing good for humanity and the planet."

[29] **What would Marie Kondo do**. Carmina Masoliver writes, "Marie Kondo is an organising consultant, author and TV presenter who helps people to de-clutter by asking if items 'spark joy'. I wrote this poem whilst pausing my ironing, as the lines came to me whilst ironing a dress I can no longer fit into, which is currently still in my wardrobe. Mare Kondo would not be happy."

[30] **Aura**. Wayne Paul Mattingly writes that this is, "A very quick snapshot into the moment before epileptic seizure." Queried about the full-stop (American English: "period") between the two stanzas, Wayne Mattingly replied, "Yes, I would like to retain the period between the stanzas. It's simply a conventional punctuation mark used in an unconventional manner—given its own line, to conclude the stanza.

(And "formally" separate it from the following stanza which begins each line with a capital letter.)"

[31] **Calendar Walls And Green Circles**. Wayne Paul Mattingly writes, "In this poem I think it's all in the poem."

[32] **Ocean Beach**. Wayne Paul Mattingly writes that this is, "A poem for those of us who loved San Francisco so before the techies of Silicon Valley changed it forever."

[33] **You Trees**. Jack Mayer writes, "As I learn more about trees, I am humbled by their beauty, their quiet elegance and persistence. Knowing how trees 'talk' to each other through underground networks of mycelia gives me a sense of camaraderie with the forests. When I hike in the wilderness, I now speak to the trees and feel their unique presence."

[34] **Music**. Lily Mayo writes, "Sometimes expressing emotions is difficult, so let music ease your mind, and the lyrics will spill from you. Whatever you need to say will come, just like the next verse in your favorite song."

[35] **The day I see every day**. Keith Nunes writes, "Clearly, we are all affected by the invasion of Ukraine and my poem has its origins in the horror of war. But there are also other aspects, civilian crime atrocities that occur, involving killings. This poem is an homage also to war photographers who suffer PTSD after seeing and photographing frightful sights."

[36] **Pietà**. Denise O'Hagan writes, "This poem draws its inspiration from the Pieta painted by Pietro Perugino, the Italian Renaissance painter whose compositions are well known for their classicism and formal symmetry. Like the Michelangelo sculpture of the same name, Perugino's painting depicts the Virgin Mary mourning over the body of her son. Executed around 1483 -1493, it was originally painted for the church of San Giusto alle Mura, outside Florence, and is now housed in the Uffizi.

Notes

Nicodemus, a wealthy member of the Sanhedrin who studied with Jesus, assisted in his burial, supplying myrrh and aloes as embalming spices.

Joseph of Arimathea, a disciple of Jesus, is known as being the man who obtained permission from Pontius Pilate to remove the body of Jesus after his crucifixion, and purchased linen in which to bury him.

[37] **Matariki**. Helen Oliver provides the following.

Notes

Matariki In Maori culture in Aotearoa New Zealand, Matariki celebrates the first rising of the Matariki star cluster (also known as the Pleiades) after a hiatus when it is not visible. Matariki signals the MÄori new year at the beginning of the lunar calendar. This year, for the first time ever, Matariki was celebrated as a public holiday, acknowledging the importance and deep meaning of this occasion.

The kōwhai is a native tree with dangling yellow flowers. As well as signalling spring, it can be seen as a symbol of personal growth and a nudge to let go the past and face the future with renewed energy and hope.

[38] **Never Enough...** Helen Oliver tells us that she, "was prompted to write this by a Proverse theme a couple of years ago but didn't complete it in time to submit it!"

[39] **reflections at the end of the day**. Helen Oliver writes, "This poem arose literally as described, watching the flames of my winter fire and realising the resemblance to certain relationships I was aware of."

[40] **Soul**. Helen Oliver writes, "Someone challenged me to explain the difference between self, spirit and soul. At a loss at first, after thinking more deeply, I wrote this poem."

[41] **After the Argument**. Rena Ong writes, "This Ghazal reflects my observation of silences or non-communication in

some long-standing relationships. The need for re-connecting. The desire to make an effort to rebuild that which has temporarily broken."

[42] **Spilt Milk**. Rena Ong writes, "The use of the word 'wall' in the poem shows its many functions for the woman in this story. First of safety and then surrendering her defences through love and finally being broken. In the end, despite the safety of the wall and its shards of glass added for protection, it is not enough for the woman in this poem to feel safe within and she has in fact ended being cut by the very thing she thought protected her."

[43] **Wordle**. Jun Pan writes, "The poem was inspired by the popular word game Wordle, using all five letter-words from a randomly generated Wordle word. Despite the limitations of the five-letter word, the poem conveys unique emotions and ideas, inviting the reader to see language in a new light."

[44] **How The Fish Feel**. Joanna Radwańska-Williams writes, "When in China, I was fascinated by the habit of keeping fish and other seafood live in an aquarium in restaurants. I felt for the poor fish swimming there oblivious to the fact that any minute, they might be fished out, cooked and eaten by happy customers. This poem does a Gestalt switch of perspective - in my imagination, I become the fish."

[45] **Singing in the Messiah**. Joanna Radwańska-Williams writes, "This poem was inspired by a performance of Handel's Messiah. In the programme notes, I read that the countertenor had once been a baritone but had accidentally discovered another voice within himself one day - I think it was when he shrieked in the dressing room because he had cut himself while shaving, and another singer remarked that he could be a countertenor! Can you imagine, one day discovering within yourself the voice of an angel? As an audience member, I was 'silently mouthing the words' because I had the desire to sing along with the singers. Performances of Handel's Messiah sometimes invite the audience to sing along."

[46] **The Colour of Water**. Joanna Radwańska-Williams writes, "Water sustains life. I love water. I love walking on a beach; in my childhood I loved swimming in a river. In this poem, the water in my bath reminds me of all the amazing watery places on this Earth."

[47] **we few**. kerry rawlinson explains that this, "is a mirror poem, reflecting (in a literal sense) on who or what institutions or entities control us. As with most things in life, often a different viewpoint offers a completely novel experience; an opening; a way forward. Sometimes, as in the poem's title, life is a palindrome and turns out the same whether you experience it forwards—or backwards."

[48] **facing the impossible**. Melissa Reed writes, "This poem transpires during the final ceremony of a Lunar New Year in Nanjing, China—the Lanterns and Rituals Ceremony—when we light and float candles representing our planted seeds of peace and reconciliation to be harvested at the Mid-Autumn Moon Festival."

[49] **Epiphany**. Allegra Jostad Silberstein writes, "Spring for me is always a time of renewal".

[50] **Recovery and Renewal**. Wesley Sims writes, "I know women who were raped. It can be a long hard road back to feeling healthy and whole; some struggle for many years to recover. I wrote a poem about a woman who was raped. One assault victim suggested I also write about the struggle and process for recovery and renewal. Thus I have written this poem."

[51] **Alone in Germany**. Abbie Taylor writes, "A participant in my local poetry group spends part of the year in Germany with her husband, who tours all over the country and plays the cello. Last year, each of us in the group wrote a poem inspired by her situation and emailed it to her. I believe this cheered her up considerably."

⁵² **In The Bowling Alley**. Abbie Taylor writes, "In college, I was required to take a couple of semesters of physical education. Because of my visual impairment, whenever I took such a class in the past, I either fell flat on my face while running or got hit in the face with a ball. So, I thought bowling would give me the least chance of being injured. The instructor, taking pity on me, arranged for me to bowl on a lane all by myself. She worked with me to improve my skill until that day when I finally bowled a strike."

⁵³ **Now That You're Gone**. Abbie Taylor writes, "I wrote this poem in 2015, ten years after my late husband and I were married and three years after he passed. Every detail is pretty much true today."

⁵⁴ **Watching the Dusk on a Rainy Night: Musing**. Luisa Ternau writes that this poem, "is inspired by the natural world. It is a meditation on memories, and their eventual transformation into something positive."

⁵⁵ **Upsala Glacier**. Edward Tiesse writes, "When traveling in Argentina just prior to the pandemic, I hiked beneath what is left of the Upsala Glacier. I was overcome with its beauty but deeply saddened with its demise. I am heart broken by what we are doing to our planet and tried to express this in my poem."

⁵⁶ **Morning Mist**. Anna Verhaegh writes that this poem, "came to me one early autumn/winter morning and I had the inspiration to just write. It started with one line, but it grew into a poem that captures and transports you into another world of fantasy—an airy-fairy, floaty, feely kind of thing. A relaxing and meditative poem to get you started in your day."

⁵⁷ **Ma-ly**. Honghua Wang writes, "'Ma-ly' is about June submerged in a multitude of events in the author's life including the selection of a primary school, illness, weather and music practice."

[58] **Unfolding 2022**. Honghua Wang writes, "As the name implies, 'Unfolding 2022', describes what happened in the year 2022. It reveals the sudden and seamless change of our life from the ordinary to the new normal as well as people's attitudes towards it."

[59] **Lot and His Daughters**. George Watt writes, "The story of Lot's escape from Sodom is well-known—traditionally used to show how an obedient man is saved from destruction, and a disobedient wife is punished when she does look back at the destruction of Sodom after being told not to. She is, for her efforts, turned into a pillar of salt. Christian Sunday schools all over the world relate this story to encourage good behaviour in men and obedience in women. But what is less known, and never discussed because of its worrying ambiguity is Lot's ensuing incest with his two daughters, in the cave where they seek refuge after the conflagration. I have always been intrigued (and often horrified) by the fury and pragmatism of the God of the Old Testament who, for example, demands the death sentence for violating the sabbath, cursing one's parents, or inadvertently helping one of the priestly class to undertake his duties with the Tabernacle. He even commands the slaughter of the whole population of towns that are under siege. This dramatic monologue, where the reader is the audience, uses Lot and his thinking to highlight the terrible ambiguities at the heart of his story."

[60] **Honest Toil**. Michael Witts writes, "This poem tells a simple story simply. Its unadorned form mirrors the work of the farmer."

[61] **Of The Floating World**. Michael Witts writes, "This poem is in part an ekphrasis of that ubiquitous Hokusai print and a musing on the process involved in ukiyo-e prints. Prints of the 'Great Wave' are everywhere but the fact is no two prints are exactly the same.

One of the original set of prints from the 1830s is in the British Museum. Recently I visited the Hokusai museum outside Nagano Japan where further prints, complete and incomplete, are housed together with the original wooden blocks for each of the layers of the print. I was struck by the way in which the process of producing a print degrades the wood block, the way in which the act of creation carries with it decay.

When looking at this work the connections to comics and Pop Art are obvious. This is probably why it still resonates today. The wave dominates. But it is there to tell the story. We know it is morning because of the way the sun breaks through the summer storm. We know the boats are heading out to sea because they are travelling right to left across the page. They may be trapped in the storm but they are heading out of Kanagawa Bay not running back to shelter. In the foreground the conical shapes of the waves and clouds mirror that of Mt Fuji in the background. The waves are there to frame Mt Fuji. The dynamic foreground emphasises the constancy of Mt Fuji in the centre. This is the first of a series of 36 studies of Mt Fuji completed by the artist."

[62] **Transmogrification.** Michael Witts writes, "This poem came about after an extended period of summer rain brought the pond at home to life with the sound of frog-call. The cauldron erupted into life. The poem was written with the theme of 'renewal' in mind.—The life cycle accelerated by the rain.—Then just as quickly the frogs were gone.

I wanted to use 'transmrogify' [*sic*] in the poem but only managed to prove to myself it was a word I could not use, and furthermore, one I could not spell. Hence it got banished to the title."

Mingled Voices 7

SOME POETRY AND POETRY COLLECTIONS
Published by Proverse Hong Kong

A Gateway Has Opened, by Liam Blackford. 2021.

Alphabet, by Andrew S. Guthrie.2015.

Astra and Sebastian, by L.W. Illsley. 2011.

Black Holes Within Us, by Marta Markoska.2021.

Bliss of Bewilderment, by Birgit Bunzel Linder. 2017.

The Burning Lake, by Jonathan Locke Hart. 2016.

Celestial Promise, by Hayley Ann Solomon. 2017.

Chasing light,by Patricia GlintonMeicholas. 2013.

China suite and other poems,
by Gillian Bickley. 2009.

Entanglements: Physics, love, and wilderness dreams by Jack
Mayer

Epochal Reckonings,by J.P. Linstroth, 2020.

For the record and other poems of Hong Kong,
by Gillian Bickley. 2003.

Frida Kahlo's cry and other poems,
by Laura Solomon. 2015.

Grandfather's Robin, by Gillian Bickley, 2020.

Heart to Heart: Poems, by Patty Ho. 2010.

H/ERO/T/IC BOOK, by Marta Markoska 2020.

Mingled Voices 7

Home, away, elsewhere,
by Vaughan Rapatahana. 2011.

Hong Kong Growing Pains, by Jon Ng.2020.

Immortelle and bhandaaraa poems,
by LelawatteeManoo-Rahming. 2011.

In vitro, by Laura Solomon. 2nd ed. 2014.

Irreverent poems for pretentious people,
by Henrik Hoeg. 2016.

The layers between (essays and poems),
by Celia Claase. 2015.

Of leaves & ashes, by Patty Ho.2016.

Life Lines, by Shahilla Shariff. 2011.

*Mingled voices: the international Proverse Poetry Prize
anthology 2016*, edited by Gillian and Verner Bickley.2017.

*Mingled voices 2: the international Proverse Poetry Prize
anthology 2017*, edited by Gillian and Verner Bickley.2018.

*Mingled voices 3: the international Proverse Poetry Prize
anthology 2018*, edited by Gillian and Verner Bickley.2019.

*Mingled voices 4: the international Proverse Poetry Prize
anthology 2019*, edited by Gillian and Verner Bickley.2020.

*Mingled voices 5: the international Proverse Poetry Prize
anthology 2020*, edited by Gillian and Verner Bickley.2021.

*Mingled voices 6: the international Proverse Poetry Prize
anthology 2021*, edited by Gillian and Verner Bickley.2022.

Moving house and other poems from Hong Kong,
by Gillian Bickley. 2005.

Mingled Voices 7

Over the Years: Selected Collected Poems, 1972-2015,
by Gillian Bickley. 2017.

Painting the borrowed house: poems, by Kate Rogers. 2008.

Perceptions, by Gillian Bickley. 2012.

Please Stand Back from the Platform Door, by Vishal Nanda.
2021.

Poems from the Wilderness, by Jack Mayer, 2020.

Rain on the pacific coast, by Elbert Siu Ping Lee. 2013.

refrain, by Jason S. Polley. 2010.

Savage Charm, by Ahmed Elbeshlawy. 2019.

Seeking Solace, by Nikhil Parekh. 2022.

Shadow play, by James Norcliffe. 2012.

Shadows in deferment, by Birgit Bunzel Linder. 2013.

Shifting sands, by Deepa Vanjani. 2016.

*Sightings: a collection of poetry, with an essay, 'communicating
poems'*, by Gillian Bickley. 2007.

Smoked pearl: poems of Hong Kong and beyond,
by Akin Jeje (Akinsola Olufemi Jeje). 2010.

Of symbols misused, by Mary-Jane Newton. 2011.

The Hummingbird Sometimes Flies Backwards, by D.J.
Hamilton. 2019.

The Year of the Apparitions, by José Manuel Sevilla. 2020.

Twilight Language, by Vinita Agrawal. 2022.

Mingled Voices 7

Uncharted Waters by Paola Caronni. 2021.

Unlocking, by Mary-Jane Newton. March 2014.

Violet, by Carolina Ilica. March 2019.

Wonder, lust & itchy feet, by Sally Dellow. 2011.

Mingled Voices 7

www.ingramcontent.com/pod-product-compliance
Lightning Source LLC
Chambersburg PA
CBHW071609150726
48000CB00004B/1642